FIFTY PLUS

FIFTY PLUS

A Boomer's Guide to
Health and Well-Being

Othniel J. Seiden, MD

TAYLOR PUBLISHING COMPANY
Dallas, Texas

Published by Taylor Publishing Company
1550 West Mockingbird Lane
Dallas, Texas 75235

Library of Congress Cataloging-in-Publication Data

Seiden, Othniel J.
    50 plus : a boomer's guide to health and well-being / Othniel J.
Seiden.
        p.   cm.
    ISBN 0-87833-943-4
    1. Middle aged persons—Health and hygiene. 2. Aged—Health
and hygiene. 3. Longevity. I. Title.
    RA777.5.S44 1997
    610.'0434—dc21   96-52139
                                                    CIP

Printed in the United States of America

10 9 8 7 6 5 4 3 2 1

This book I dedicate to my mother, Julia Seiden, who at ninety-one is still traveling all over the world, enjoying concert series, and spending time with her nine great-grandchildren. She is setting a healthy, happy, active example for us all.

Contents

ONE

May You Live To Be 120

Virtually all recent medical research on aging points to the fact that the human animal, you and me included, has the potential to live for up to 120 years. That means 120 active, happy, and productive years—not years in a rocking chair, wheel chair, or nursing home. That being the case, the second half of our lives doesn't even begin until sixty. However, since most of us have spent the first part of our lives mistreating our God-given equipment, this human body of ours, we may not all make it to 120. But the good news is that most of us should be able to make it to one hundred and well over. This book is dedicated to giving us the best possible chance to reach our true life potential. Let's re-emphasize, we are talking about healthy, happy, active, and productive years full of the things we enjoy doing. We are talking about adding years to our lives and, more important, putting quality life in our remaining years.

How often have you heard the question, "If you had it to do over again, what would you change?" Well, if you are coming up on fifty, theoretically, you *do* have it all to do over again. Just think what you should be able to do with those years, knowing all that you've learned in the first fifty! What you need to do is get yourself into the best shape you can so that you can live out as much of your 120-year potential as possible. It is to that end that this book is committed. Follow the program outlined in this book and within a year, you should be as fit as you can be and headed for as bright and long a future as possible. May you live to 120!

Still a little skeptical about all those studies that say we should be full of fun, vigor, and productive activity to 120 years of age? Let's just look around at what's going on in the rest of the world—and not too far from home, I might add. It might surprise you to know just how many people over one hundred years of age are living right here in the United States. Would you believe over 36,000? That's 16,000 more than just ten years ago, and that number is expected to pass 75,000 by the year 2000. We've learned a lot about aging in the past decade. And the best part of our statistics are showing that Americans are not only living longer, but also are developing fewer disabilities and chronic diseases. In fact, our aging population is becoming more robust by the year. Older Americans are more active than ever before; they're hiking, biking, traveling, turning to second careers, returning to classes, and pursuing college degrees. As these people enter their sixties, seventies, and even eighties, they are turning their backs on the rocking chair and nursing home. Retirement communities today plan full schedules of vigorous mental and physical activity programs, and more of their members are living on their own. But this kind of longevity is not new. In other parts of the world people have been living remarkably long lives for years.

I work as medical director of the organizations

Volunteers to the World and Doctors to the World, which send volunteers, both nonmedical and medical personnel, all over the world to areas in need. This gives me the opportunity to go to some fascinating places, most of them in the Third World. It was a surprise to me that health in the Third World is often better than it is here at home.

We've all heard of the starvation and terrible diseases in places like India, Bangladesh, Somalia, and the Sudan, but in reality, these are exceptions to the rule. These situations make the news—as well they should—to arouse our interest and inspire us to give aid. Less frequently do we hear about the Third World people who live nine to ten decades or longer—active and productive decades.

One of my first exposures to these long-living Third World people was in one of the most primitive places on earth, Zona Miskita, Honduras. Life in this area goes on pretty much as it has, unchanged, for more than six hundred years. The area has few roads and virtually no electricity or other modern technology. I was among people who had never seen a modern doctor, having been cared for by Medicine Chiefs when they were ill. Herbs, teas, and potions were the main medicines of the area. Nevertheless, many of these people remained active into their late nineties.

Further examples of people I have worked with who live longer, more active lives than most Americans are the inhabitants of Barbuda, a small island in the Caribbean just thirty miles due north of Antigua. The island has only about 1,200 residents, all living in one small village at the edge of a large lagoon. Their only medical care is provided by volunteer doctors who rotate to the island a month at a time. But even before we provided them with volunteer medical care, these people were living into their nineties and past one hundred, and as in Honduras, they remained active and productive.

In Ecuador I was introduced to real longevity. I was with a team of ophthalmologists and nurses, volunteers who replaced three hundred cataracts with intra-ocular lenses. My job was to examine all the patients to make sure they were able to withstand surgery. I also examined numerous others who were there for other eye treatments. Altogether I checked more than five hundred of the natives of that area high in the Andes mountains, at an altitude of about 10,000 feet. Among them, I found no heart disease, no cancer, no diabetes, no evidence of stroke or hypertension, all the diseases that commonly kill off Americans in our fifth, sixth, and seventh decades of life. I was examining natives in their thirties to their nineties, and even as old as 100, 102, 106, and one as old as 114. And these people were leading active lives, most having walked several miles to come to our hospital in the town of Garanda. Furthermore, I was told we were not too far from a village in which people routinely lived over 100 years—to 130 or more.

Armenia is another country deprived of our high-tech medical system whose people suffer severe economic hardships. I was privileged to lead one of two American medical teams into that country immediately after its dev-astating earthquake of 1988. In the major city of Yeravan, life expectancy did not seem any different than ours. There the people were exposed to pollution and stress equal to that in any of our major cities. They smoked and ate high-fat diets beyond even our levels of indulgence. The only area that showed an appreciable improvement over the habits of most Americans was their slightly less sedentary lifestyle. But outside their capital city it was quite another story. In the mountain villages, the diet was considerably healthier, the air cleaner, the lifestyle more relaxed, and tobacco use virtually unknown. There people walked several miles a day to get from one place to another, and not surprisingly, people lived long active lives. Ages into the late 90s and up to 110 years are not uncommon; 120 to 130 are less common but not unheard of, and the oldest recorded age of 147 came from that area.

The point is that we Americans are living only one-half to two-thirds of our allotted time on this earth, and we aren't fit enough to fully enjoy the years that we do survive. The good news is that we can do something about it. We can begin by emulating those peoples who already live ten or more active, healthy decades. When we examine their lives, we can see four aspects of healthy living common to them all: good nutrition, exercise, lack of exposure to environmental poisons, and minimal distress. These are the categories we must concentrate on to reach our own full potential for health and longevity, and fortunately, the changes we have to make in our lifestyles aren't drastic or painful. Whether you have just turned fifty or you're much older, making these changes now will help extend your life and enhance its quality.

This book will lead you through these changes. Make them and you'll be amazed at how much health, activity, fun, productivity, and ambition can be restored to your life. Your goal, "should you accept this assignment," is to become as fit as you can possibly be by this time next year, heading for a bright and long, happy, healthy, active, and productive future.

TWO

Motivation: Your Key to Success

If this program fails for you it is not because you can't stick to it or that it won't work for you; it's because you're not motivated enough. Motivation makes the difference. If you aren't dedicated enough to make the simple lifestyle changes required to live a long, full, active life, you'll fail for sure. However, if your health means enough to you, you'll make and stick by the few simple changes suggested here, and your success will be assured.

You must have some motivation to get back into shape or you wouldn't have bought this book. Of course, "get *back* into shape," presupposes that you once were in shape at all. That's not necessarily true. Many Americans are very out of shape and have been that way since childhood. Well, it's never too late to get into good shape—even if you've never been there before. You need not concentrate on your past. It's from this day forward that you should worry about. Follow the program in this book, and a year from now you can be in the best condition you've been in years—or ever—regardless of your age. Because the only thing that might be standing in the way is lack of motivation, let's build on the bit of motivation that got you to buy this book and begin reading.

One of the strongest motivations for you to get into and stay in shape is that if you don't, it's a downhill slide for you from this point to the grave. Either you make an effort to improve yourself, or next year at this time—and every succeeding year—you're going to be fatter, flabbier, and weaker, and you'll have less endurance, resistance to sickness, and appeal to others.

Nothing can keep you from aging, but the process can be slowed. Your physical aging need not speed ahead of your chronological age or even keep up with it. No one can guarantee you'll live any longer because you're in good shape and physical condition, but authorities on aging and longevity would all bet you would. And I guarantee you'll enjoy the rest of your life a lot more if you maintain your physical and mental health—that is what this book is really all about.

Getting into your best possible physical condition will require four main activities: correcting your nutritional status, establishing your walking program, reducing your stress/distress ratio, and getting rid of a few bad habits you may have picked up. To do these things you'll have to establish some goals. Setting goals is not that difficult, and this book will help you to set realistic targets for yourself. Continuing to work toward those goals, however, is another matter. Motivation is what will determine your success or failure.

Fortunately, your ability to stick to your new program doesn't depend solely on your reserve of will power. Forming new, healthy habits is not that difficult, and after a few weeks of your new lifestyle, many things will become second nature to you. So, if you can motivate yourself to stick to your new lifestyle long enough for it to become habit, the rest will be easy.

To help you through these first few weeks, think of all the reasons you might want to get into better physical condition. Make a list that you can review each day. Add to the list as new reasons suggest themselves. In case you have trouble thinking of some reasons, I suggest a few here.

I'd Like to Look Better

I can't think of anyone who wouldn't want to look more attractive. Anyone who says this reason isn't close to the top of his list of motives is probably kidding himself. It's a rare individual who cares nothing about his appearance. This can be one of the strongest forces motivating you to get into good physical condition.

Your appearance establishes the first impression when others meet you. Others draw immediate opinions about you the instant they see you, before you say a word to show them what a stunning mind and personality you really have. Whether in social, business, or family situations, if you have a poor appearance, your job of winning others over is that much more difficult. Consider how much easier it would be to attract others to your ideas, your projects, and yourself if you were in good physical condition.

I'd Like to Feel Better

Remember how much more energy you had five or ten years ago? Or maybe it was just last year. If you don't turn things around, think how rotten you'll feel next year or in five years. Either you're going to feel better than ever next year or you're going to be another year older and feel a couple years older or worse. It's not going to get better unless you do something about it now and keep working at it. If you improve your physical condition during this year, you'll begin to feel better and continue to feel better as time goes on. If, on the other hand, you continue in the direction you've been headed, you can expect to become less attractive and less energetic than ever.

Along with increased activity, endurance, and muscle tone, and with improved nutritional status and reduction of fat deposits will come feelings of well-being and energy you never thought you'd experience again.

I'd Like to Become a Better Athlete

Your aspirations don't have to be toward world-class competition; there are a lot of reasons to want to become more proficient at athletic activities you enjoy. If you improve your game, whether it's golf, bowling, cycling, racquetball, tennis, touch football, or whatever, you'll have more fun at it. Athletics doesn't mean you have to join a team, league, or expensive athletic club. Maybe you just want to be able to keep up with your kids—or parents!

I'd Like to Tone Up

Becoming a proficient athlete may be low on your priority list, but how about just firming up those loose muscles and trimming off a lot of that stored fat? If nothing else it will give you a better body to hang your clothes on. But remember, you don't have to run a daily military obstacle course—just take a brisk walk five or more days a week.

If you alter your nutritional habits a little and walk an hour a day for just five days a week, you'll remove about a pound of fat from your body each week. Think that isn't a lot? Go out into the kitchen and see how big a one pound can of cooking fat or butter is. A pound of cooking lard and your own body fat are about the same in volume and quality. Now imagine how much better you'll feel when about twenty-five of those come off your body mass.

I Need to Lose Some Weight for Business

There is no doubt that you'll meet the public better, earn the respect of colleagues easier, and impress your superiors more if you look better and have more energy, vigor, and endurance. You'll do a better job no matter what it is. If you don't do work that requires strength and action, remember that a mind in a healthy body functions better, clearer, faster, more efficiently, and longer.

Still need more convincing? Ask yourself this question: If there are two of us up for the same position or promotion and we're equally capable in all respects, but the other guy looks a lot sharper, who's going to get the job?

Being able to earn more money can be a strong motivator!

I'm Tired of Breaking Down

It's a fact that as your body deteriorates it loses its resistance to bacteria, viruses, sprains, strains, stresses, and other maladies. You might just as well face it, your body is going to continue to deteriorate until you make a concerted effort to turn things around. There's no such thing as status quo in biology. You have to choose between working at getting better and healthier or watching yourself go to pot. If you choose the spectator role, you'll see yourself get fatter, weaker, more prone to illness, developing aches and pains, and generally turning more unattractive.

I Want to Be Sexually Attractive

Sex is important to everyone and damned important to most of us, though some won't admit it as eagerly as others. If you're married, you probably want your spouse to feel proud to be with you. And most people want others to take positive note of them, whether they're married or not. Of course, if you're not married you probably want to make everyone's head turn. If you want to be attractive to others, your job will be easier if you get into shape. People who are healthy and fit are more attractive to everyone.

I Want to Be Stronger

Remember the old Charles Atlas ads? They sold a lot of self-improvement courses. Why? Because we all want to feel confident. It wasn't just the bulging muscles, but what those muscles represented. Many of us want to be strong even though very few of us has a goal of being a bodybuilder. For those who want that, great! Go for it! For most of us, however, just a little added strength really adds to our confidence. As your body improves, so will your self-image.

As your body builds muscle tone, others will find it harder to take advantage of you, not because they will be scared you'll punch them in the nose, but because you'll show a new confidence. People don't try to intimidate those who exude confidence.

I Want to Gain Weight

Most people who want to gain weight try to put it on by eating. Two things are wrong with that plan. First, your metabolism is probably so elevated that you'll never store any fat. Second, fat is not the kind of weight you want to add. Remember, fat doesn't weigh nearly as much as muscle or lean meat. You get muscle by exercising, not just by eating. You should look into a bodybuilding program in addition to your walking program.

I Want My Friends to Respect Me

Peer regard is perhaps the strongest motivator we have. What our friends and close acquaintances think of us is extremely important. We play different roles with our friends because we want their respect in specific ways. If they can respect our physical prowess and appearance, it is a plus to the relationship. Self-esteem depends on the esteem of others. You can't think highly of yourself if you don't think others think well of you.

I Want Praise Instead of Criticism

If you've been overweight and out of shape for some time, I'm sure you've heard your share of unkind comments—some from well-meaning persons, others from those looking for a place to dig at you where it hurts. Just as criticism is punishing, so praise is rewarding. Reward is a much stronger motivating tool than the punishment of criticism. If you're finally sick to death of the criticism, perhaps your quest for praise will drive you to the decision to improve your physical condition. Praise will drive most people to higher aspiration.

I Want to Look Younger

Humankind has been dreaming of the fountain of youth since ancient times. Of course, eternal youth is beyond the scope of this book, but renewed vigor, improved appearance, and revitalized health are not. And those are the characteristics that do spell a more youthful appearance and more self-esteem. Get back into shape, and people will comment that you are looking younger. You'll feel younger, function better, and if it makes you live longer, it's almost the same as being younger.

I Want to Be "In" with the Healthier People

To be a part of a group and to feel included are strong motivating forces. The human animal is a social creature. Most of us gravitate toward groups of people with like interests. Birds of a feather do indeed flock together. Right now you may belong to a sedentary group of dodo birds. If you'll recall, the dodo bird is a large, flightless bird that has been extinct since the seventeenth century. And in today's society, the sedentary pudgies are also becoming an extinct group. They are literally dying off at a faster rate than the slimmer, trimmer, more active folks. If you're like most people, you will want to fly with the eagles rather than wander toward extinction with the dodo birds.

My Spouse Is on My Case

Most people are concerned about their spouse's health, appearance, and welfare. That's why they want them to do something positive about their physical shape. Who can blame them? The prospect of widow- or widowerhood is not usually a bright one. If you won't shape up for yourself, maybe you'll do it for him or her.

These are but a few of the reasons people give for finally deciding to get into shape. Whatever your reasons may be, don't let them get away from you. Write them down. Keep them where you can see them easily, where you can look at them often to remind yourself. Any reason should be reason enough. Review the reasons above and add your own reasons in the space below.

_____

_____

_____

_____

_____

_____

_____

Remember, motivation is all that stands between you and your success!

THREE

Get Back into Shape

Getting back into shape implies that you were once in good shape. If you weren't as fit as you could have been in the past, it should make little difference. This exercise program should work for you as well. It is based on the exercise that is most prevalent among the people who are outliving us by three to five decades. In recent years this exercise has been discovered by our exercise physiologists and sports medicine physicians to be the most beneficial and safe aerobic exercise that men and women can participate in. Because of the primitive conditions in the areas where our long-lived counterparts reside, they walk four to twelve miles a day. Walking is the best exercise to develop a strong and healthy cardiovascular system and to keep our muscles and joints functioning well past age fifty. No, you won't have to walk twelve miles every day, but a brisk walk for forty-five minutes to an hour each day will make your body stronger and healthier. Let's take a look at what a daily brisk walk will do for you.

Why A Walking Program?

Walking is aerobic. It will help reduce your body fat. It will condition your heart, lungs, and body. It will help lower your cholesterol and blood pressure. It will add years to your life and life to your years! Walking is the safest, most natural, most perfect aerobic exercise the human animal can participate in.

The simple secret to weight and body fat control is this:

- If you ingest more calories than you burn, you'll store excess body fat and your fat-to-lean body mass ratio will increase.

- If you burn off more calories than you ingest, you'll gradually burn off that stored fat to make up the needed energy and your fat-to-lean body mass ratio will decrease.

Thus, if you can increase your exercise during the day, you will also increase the amount of body fat you burn off. In addition, the exercise should tone and build muscle which increases your lean body mass. Since muscle mass burns many more calories than fat, even while at rest, your metabolic rate will increase, causing your body to use far more calories at rest or during exercise. In fact, muscle burns thirty-eight times more calories than fat even at rest, greatly increasing your body metabolism. This will favorably alter your body fat ratio and move you toward your ideal body weight. This does not necessarily mean you'll lose weight. Remember, fat is lighter than lean body tissue, and you may actually gain weight in the exchange, but it will be an exchange of healthy tissue for fat. Not a bad deal!

So what is the next step? First, talk your plan over

with your doctor. If you are recovering from a heart problem, of course, your cardiologist must be made aware of any activity you hope to undertake. If you are a spouse, friend, or relative of a heart patient and want to take advantage of this opportunity to start a lifestyle change of your own along with the patient, there are some things you should consider as well. If you have been sedentary for several years, if you are over thirty-five years of age, or if you have any chronic illness for which you are being regularly evaluated by a medical advisor, talk it over with him. If you fall into any of the above categories or haven't had a complete physical examination in the past few years, you should get a thorough physical evaluation. Your medical advisor should help you to set realistic and safe goals for yourself and help you to monitor your progress toward those goals. If there are circumstances regarding your personal health status that dictate adjustments in this program, only your personal medical advisor is qualified to help you make those adjustments.

Any exercise program you begin should be started slowly, especially if you have been sedentary for a long time. This program is no exception, but if you follow it, you'll see results in a surprisingly short time. Although changing your nutritional habits and practices should help you to improve your health and your fat-to-lean body mass ratio, such changes can't do it alone. Exercise must be a part of your new lifestyle. Exercise is vital to your good health.

The human body is adaptable—an important survival characteristic in most situations—but it works against you when you try to reduce your body fat by nutritional change only. This adaptability is why so many dieters fail when they try to lose weight only by cutting caloric intake. We humans are a part of the animal kingdom, and therefore we respond physiologically to starvation like most other animals. When other animals go into a starvation period, such as during famines or hibernation, their bodies go into a conservation mode. Their metabolism slows dramatically to conserve fat stores. The same happens when the human animal starves itself during a diet. As soon as our bodies sense that they are being deprived of their usual quantity of food and calorie intake our metabolic rate slows and our systems go into high-efficiency mode to preserve stored fat. This adds to the dieter's frustration by slowing the rate of weight loss and reduction of fat deposits.

Vigorous exercise helps to "override" our starvation defense system. Because exercise demands energy, it forces our metabolic rate to remain high. Our bodies can't go into starvation or hibernation mode. Thus, it is vitally important to exercise along with any nutritional changes we make in our eating habits.

In addition to what exercise does to help us attain our ideal body weight, recent studies have shown that exercise is essential to prolonged life. Statistics now conclusively show that even minimal exercise reduces premature death from all causes. We have long advocated exercise to strengthen the cardiovascular system to reduce premature death from heart disease, but strong evidence now shows that exercise also reduces the rate of premature death from cancer, stroke, diabetes, and apparently all other disease processes and normal causes of early death. And although the exact mechanism by which exercise will prolong life is not fully understood, it only makes sense that a physically fit body will resist illness and injury more effectively and, when illness or injury does occur, heal faster and more completely.

You will benefit from as little exercise as forty-five

minutes of brisk walking three times a week. Although that's a great start, this program encourages you to work up to taking a brisk walk for an hour a day, five to seven days a week. That may sound rough to you right now, especially if you've been a sedentary person in the recent past, but it will pay off in more ways than you can imagine. Once you get into your workout program, you won't think it is tough at all. In the next chapter, we will work you into your exercise program, and you'll be back in good physical condition before you know it.

If you've been a sedentary person, the idea of starting an exercise program may be intimidating. You see all those folks out there jogging, running marathons, biking, playing tennis and racquetball, and participating in triathalons. You say you want no part of all that pain and effort. I have good news for you. The "no pain, no gain" bit is a myth. The exercise program this book advocates is based strictly on walking. That's not to say you can't participate in other exercise activities. On the contrary, I recommend that you participate in as many exercise or athletic activities as you desire—but the other activities should not replace your walking program. Walking is an absolute must!

Regardless of which other activities you participate in, none can replace your walking program's benefit to your physical and mental well-being. This statement will be fully explained and defended in the next chapter. The fact is that walking is humankind's most perfect aerobic exercise. Walking is all the exercise you need to become physically fit and stay that way for the rest of your life. Other exercise activities can benefit you in other ways, but none can replace a good walking program for total conditioning: not biking, swimming, running, jogging, tennis, racquetball, aerobic dance, or calisthenics. Only cross-country skiing is potentially better for you than a walking program, but only if you live where you can cross-country ski daily all year.

A walking program has the additional advantage of being accessible to everyone almost anywhere. It requires no special equipment, club membership, expensive investment, or special clothing other than comfortable shoes, and special athletic skills are not a requirement. If you are one of the rare individuals who has an illness that prevents brisk walking, then alternative aerobic activities will be suggested for you in the next chapter.

For those of you who might be skeptical of the benefits of walking as a sole (no pun intended) exercise program, consider the following:

- Walking is humankind's most natural exercise for individuals at any age. Of all exercises, it is the safest and least traumatic to body and joints. We've been designed to walk great distances at remarkable speeds. Running was meant only for short spurts during emergencies. We weren't designed to withstand the punishment of long continuous running or jogging, which requires lifting the body weight completely off the ground and landing on bent knees with each jarring stride.

- Walking exercises the entire body and mind. It uses the upper body more than running and the legs far more than swimming. In a vigorous, brisk walk there is virtually no muscle group in your body at rest. And as you will learn later, walking stimulates mental and creative activity and reduces distress.

- Walking will develop your endurance within safe boundaries faster than any other aerobic sport.

No other sport can provide you with the benefits you will be getting from your walking program in as short a time as a week from now.

- Your walking program will give you the best cardiovascular/cardiopulmonary workout you can get and with the greatest margin of safety.

- Walking can be done by virtually anyone, anytime, anywhere. It is probably the most indulged in sport in the world. Over forty percent of Americans will tell you that walking is their main source of exercise—and Americans are newcomers to the sport.

- Walking is a family sport, one of the few that all ages can participate in together as equals.

- We call walking a sport because it is a competitive event even at the Olympic level if you want to pursue it. Race walking is becoming popular throughout the United States as it has been in other parts of the world for decades. Contests are usually broken down into age groups so competition can be pursued at all ages into the eighties and older. Races are also divided into men's and women's divisions and are usually broken down into five, ten, thirty, and fifty kilometer events. It is interesting to note that an Olympic or World Class race walker is among the best conditioned of all athletes.

- If you're not interested in that kind of competition—and most of us aren't—the competition you'll have against yourself will be all you need to keep you going toward ever increasing goals.

- You'll probably burn more calories, exercise your heart and lungs better, imporve your circulation more, lose more weight, and develop your body and mind further by walking than you could with any other activity. In addition, walking will lower your blood pressure, reduce stress and cholesterol levels, and take off up to one pound of fat a week even if you don't alter your eating habits.

Sound too good to be true? The book I wrote with Bob Carlson, *Health Walk*, lists the following as benefits of walking:

1. It reduces the likelihood of cardiovascular and cerebrovascular disease by increasing the size of blood vessels and improving blood flow to all parts of the body.

2. It strengthens the muscles of the body, including the heart muscle, and makes them work more efficiently.

3. It slows the heart rate by increasing the stroke volume (the volume of blood the heart is able to pump with one contraction).

4. It tends to reduce the height to which arterial pressure rises during exercise and stress.

5. It encourages collateral circulation to the heart muscle. This can dramatically increase your chances of surviving a coronary occlusion (blockage of a heart artery).

6. It reduces deposits of stored fat.

7. It improves digestion and elimination of body wastes.

8. It increases the oxygen supply to the brain, increasing mental sharpness and facilitating creative thought processes.

9. It retards the aging process and gives you a more youthful appearance.

10. It aids lymphatic circulation and blood circulation in general.

11. It stimulates the metabolism, allowing you to burn calories for hours after you've stopped exercising.

12. It increases respiratory capacity.

13. It benefits tissue regeneration and recovery from trauma.

14. It reduces triglyceride (blood fat) levels.

15. It reduces insomnia and provides for better relaxation.

16. It reduces the incidence of minor illnesses, allergies, headaches, and abdominal problems.

17. It improves coordination by activating neurotransmitters and training muscle fibers.

18. It increases flexibility of joints and muscles and thus reduces aches and pains in the back, neck, and other body joints.

19. It circulates more oxygen to all body tissues.

20. It tones up the glandular systems and increases thyroid gland output.

21. It increases the production of red blood cells by the bone marrow.

22. It increases the ability to store and use reserve nutrients, which increases endurance.

23. It augments the alkaline reserve of the body, which can be significant in an emergency requiring extended effort.

24. It increases muscular strength by toning all the body muscles.

25. It counteracts feelings of fatigue.

26. It aids chemical actions that increase the potential of body cells.

27. It causes muscles to move vital fluids throughout the body, which lessens the work done by the heart.

28. It has stabilizing and normalizing effects on blood pressure.

29. It causes the release of endorphins, the body's own tranquilizers.

30. It has a hardening and strengthening effect on bones of the entire skeletal system.

31. It provides a reserve of body strength and physical efficiency.

32. It improves the ratio between high-density and low-density components of cholesterol, which lessens the risk of artery disease and many cancers.

33. It greatly improves mental outlook, optimism, morale, and self-esteem.

So there you are. With all that walking can do for you, you can't help but improve your physical and mental status. The time to begin turning your life around is now. Step number one is to speak with your personal medical advisor and discuss your intentions with her. Take this book with you and get her input. Let her help you to set some realistic goals. And start walking!

FOUR

Managing Your Aerobic Workout

I've already said that walking is the best aerobic exercise you can participate in. You might at this point ask, "What is an aerobic exercise?" *Aerobic* means "with air" and refers to activities that require increased oxygen, such as running, swimming, cycling, and walking. When you do an aerobic exercise, your heart and lungs must work harder to get extra oxygen to your muscles. Anaerobic exercises, on the other hand, do not require extra oxygen. Such activities include weightlifting, wrestling, and sprinting. They generally involve short spurts of action and use up energy stored in the muscles as fuel. While these activities certainly have benefits, they do not strengthen your heart and lungs as aerobic exercises can.

Exercise physiologists have shown that to get maximum benefit from an aerobic exercise program you must maintain your ideal exercise pulse rate for at least forty-five minutes—preferably for one hour. In addition, you should exercise enough to burn at least 2,000 calories per week, exercising at least five, and if possible, seven days a week. Walking is the best, and in most cases, the only exercise we can do to fill these requirements. There are very few, if any, other exercises most of us can keep up for forty-five minutes, much less for a full hour, while maintaining our ideal exercise pulse rate. But by walking briskly, most of us can accomplish just that. If you can't do it now, you will be able to with just a few weeks of conditioning.

When you walk a mile on level ground, regardless of the speed with which you do it, you will burn off about 100 calories. So, if you walk four miles in one hour, you'll be burning off 400 calories each day. In only five days you will burn your 2,000-calorie weekly quota. If you walk six or seven days, that's all the better. If you walk a full hour, you can maintain your ideal exercise pulse rate for over forty-five minutes and still allow for a warm up and cool down period. I can think of no other exercise that so perfectly meets all these physiological criteria for a good aerobic workout.

Your Ideal Exercise Pulse Rate

Before you can begin your exercise program, you must establish your ideal exercise pulse rate. The first step is taking your pulse. The two easiest places to count it are the wrist (either one) and the neck (either side). For the wrist or *radial* pulse, lightly place your index and middle fingers on the thumb side of the wrist with the palm of the hand facing you. You will feel a tendon just to the thumb side of the middle of your wrist. Now move your two fingertips to the thumb side of that tendon, between it and the thumb edge of your wrist. At that location begin to gradually increase the pressure you press down with until you begin to feel the pounding of your pulse. Adjust the position and pressure until you can best feel it. To count the pulse you can count each beat for one minute, or count each beat for thirty seconds and multiply by two, or count fifteen seconds and multiply by four. Do not count for one second and multiply by 60!

To take the pulse at the neck, or *carotid* pulse, put the same two fingers at the angle of your jaw. If you raise your chin, you will feel a muscle in your neck just below the angle of your jaw. Gently press your two fingers in front of that muscle where it crosses the lower edge of your jaw. You should feel the beat of the carotid artery. Now adjust the location and pressure of your fingers until you can best feel and count. Use the same math as above.

Now let's determine your ideal exercise pulse rate. Your personal rate is determined by your age.

Your ideal exercise pulse rate =
220 – your age × .7

So, if you are 65 years old, your ideal exercise
pulse rate would be as follows:

220 – 65 = 155
155 × .7 = 108

Your ideal exercise pulse rate would be 108 beats per minute. So, you would want to walk at a speed that would maintain your pulse at 108 beats per minute for forty-five minutes to one hour.

There are three other pulse rate figures you should know: your minimum exercise pulse rate, your maximum exercise pulse rate, and your resting pulse rate.

Your minimum exercise pulse rate =
220 – your age × .6

Your maximum exercise pulse rate =
220 – your age × .8

If you are 65 years of age your minimum exercise pulse rate would be 155 times .6, or 93 beats per minute, and your maximum exercise pulse rate would be 155 times .8, or 124 beats per minute.

If you take your pulse while exercising and find that your pulse rate is less than your minimum exercise pulse rate, you need to walk faster or your exercise will do you little aerobic good. If you are walking so fast that your pulse is beating faster than your maximum exercise pulse rate, you should slow your pace enough to drop below that number. So if you are 65 years of age, you should try to walk fast enough to keep your pulse between 93 and 124 beats per minute for forty-five minutes to an hour, preferably at 108 to 115 beats per minute.

Before we talk about resting pulse rate, find your minimum, maximum, and ideal exercise pulse rates in the table below and memorize them.

Table of Exercising Pulse Rates (EPR)

AGE	MINIMUM EPR	IDEAL EPR	MAXIMUM EPR
20-30	114 - 120	133 - 140	152 - 160
30-40	108 - 114	125 - 133	144 - 152
40-50	102 - 108	119 - 125	136 - 144
50-55	99 - 102	115 - 119	132 - 136
55-60	96 - 99	112 - 115	128 - 132
60-65	93 - 96	108 - 112	124 - 128
AGE	MINIMUM EPR	IDEAL EPR	MAXIMUM EPR
65-70	90 - 93	105 - 108	120 - 124
70-75	87 - 90	101 - 105	116 - 120
75-80	84 - 87	98 - 101	112 - 116
80-85	81 - 84	94 - 94	108 - 112
85-90	78 - 81	91 - 94	104 - 108
90 plus	75	90	104

Resting Pulse Rate

Your resting pulse rate will be one of your best measures of cardiovascular improvement as you progress in your walking program. To determine your resting pulse rate, take it first thing upon awakening in the morning before you get out of bed. If you can't take it then, count it after sitting or lying down completely relaxed for about ten minutes. Try to take it at the same time and under the same conditions each day. As you get into better condition, your resting pulse will become lower and lower. Other measures of your improvement are discussed in the chapter, "Weights and Measures."

Your Exercise Program

Now let's get back to your exercise goal—to develop your cardiovascular/cardiopulmonary health so you can walk an hour at your own ideal exercise pulse rate and achieve and maintain your best fitness potential.

Decide with your physician what your beginning level of exercise should be. If in doubt, start out with a minimal walk. Do what you know you can do even if it is only a short distance. If you do it with more ease than you expected, add a little distance with each walk you take. Even if you're just getting out of a sick bed and your walks are only a few feet, do them as often in the day as you can. Your walking program will progress at a much faster pace than you can imagine. Until you can walk for twenty minutes without stopping, don't feel you have to push yourself too far beyond comfort. The important thing is to make each walk a little further and/or a little faster than the last and to walk every day. Make it part of your daily routine, preferably at the same time each day. It has to be scheduled to give it its proper priority among all the other things you do each day. In fact, it has to be at the very top of your priorities. Realize that any day you don't find time to walk, you're saying that everything you do that day is more important than your health. But your health is your most important asset!

To help you measure your progress, record on paper how far you walk each day and how long it takes you. At the end of each week, compare and chart your progress. You'll be amazed at the rapid improvement. There are tables to record your progress in at the end of this book.

When you finally get to the point at which you can walk a full hour nonstop—and it will happen sooner than you or your doctor think—you should start to increase your pace a little each day until you reach your ideal exercise pulse rate. Once you reach that level, it does not mean you won't improve any more. Your physical condition will still improve gradually, and you'll know it because you'll have to walk faster over time to get your heart rate up to your ideal exercise level. So, your ideal exercise pulse rate will become another measure of your continuing cardiopulmonary health development along with your resting pulse rate.

A lot has been written about stretching and warming up before you exercise. I feel the best warm up for walking is walking. Spend the first four or five minutes of your walk gradually working up to your best exercise pace. Start out at a comfortable walk and gradually increase your stride and speed until you fall into a brisk rhythm that is adequate to give you a good cardiovascular workout.

More important than the warm up to your walk is an adequate cool down period at the end. Never, never just stop after you've been walking at your ideal exercise pulse rate or faster without cooling down with a slower walk. Reduce your speed and continue to walk until your pulse has slowed to less than your minimum exercise rate or less than 100, whichever is lower.

Then, if you want to do some stretching exercises, do them after your workout. It is amazing how often people injure themselves by overstretching while their muscles are cold and tight before their workout. If you start your walk slow and easy and build up your pace, the muscles will warm up and limber safely. Then do your stretching after the vigorous workout. You will get all the benefits of stretching without the danger of injury. Furthermore, the post-exercise stretching will keep you from getting stiff and painful muscles and joints after a vigorous workout.

For those few of you who can't walk due to a real physical handicap, the same principles apply. You must find an activity that will keep your pulse rate at its ideal exercise level for forty-five minutes to an hour. Consider swimming, rowing on a stationary rowing machine or cycling on a stationary bike. Other water exercises such as pool aerobics are also good choices. You may find that these exercises will improve your condition so that you will be able to work into a walking program after all.

As for other exercises and sports activities, they are great if you enjoy them, but they do not replace your walking program. You should participate in as many exercise or athletic activities as you enjoy, over and above your walking program. On the other hand, you need no other exercise activities other than your walking program if you don't want to do any more. It is a good idea to have some other aerobic exercises available to you for those days when you can't walk because of inclement weather or some other problem. Swimming, stationary biking, or rowing are ideal. All are good aerobic, low-impact activities.

Such activities as tennis, racquetball, baseball, and

weightlifting are anaerobic. They are wonderful activities if you enjoy them, but remember that they do not take the place of your walking program and must be done in addition to your walking. Golf and bowling are great social and stress-reducing activities and help keep your joints limber, but they are neither anaerobic nor aerobic. Again, if you enjoy them, participate in them in addition to your walking program.

A special note about weight lifting and bodybuilding: both of these activities put special stresses on the heart and vascular system, which may have a detrimental effect on some cardiovascular conditions. If you have a heart condition, be sure to get the advice of your cardiologist or cardiovascular surgeon before engaging in these activities.

Most cardiac patients benefit from limited weight programs to keep their body tone maintained. Most men shouldn't need to build muscle unless they have been sedentary for a long time. Staying toned or maintaining the strength you have is usually sufficient. Women, on the other hand, can benefit from building some strength, especially in the upper body. And here is some wonderful news: Before now, trainers have always insisted that to gain strength you had to do exercises at a weight that you could manage about a dozen repetitions of the maneuver. This is called a set. Then each set of exercises had to be repeated at least three times. Recently there have been several good studies showing that a person doing only one set of exercises developed just as fast as those doing three sets of the same exercises.

Do whatever exercises that work the muscles you want to develop or keep toned. Start with a weight that allows you to perform the exercise ten times. Do that set of exercises at least three times a week until you can do it fifteen times with about the same difficulty as the original ten you started with. Then increase the weight so that you can comfortably do the exercise about a dozen times. This will maintain your tone. If you want to build muscle, work up to fifteen times again and increase the weight again. Forget about doing multiple sets unless you want to really get into bodybuilding, in which case you should work with a trainer.

Special Consideration for Cardiac Patients

Exercise is extremely important for cardiac patients. When my father had his first heart attack more than forty years ago, he was told to reduce his activity drastically. He had to move his bedroom from the second to the first floor to avoid steps. He was told to get bed rest for a month and a half after his attack. When he was allowed to resume activity he was warned not to exert himself—ever! That was how heart disease was treated in those days. When I went to medical school a decade later, they were still advocating inactivity for heart patients. Sad to say, we were not curing heart disease, we were creating cardiac cripples.

Today we know better. The heart is a muscle. And like any muscle of the body it improves and strengthens with prudent exercise. Most important, the increased circulation of blood provides increased oxygen to nourish its hungering muscle cells. Think about this: in most cases it is a sedentary lifestyle that causes heart disease. So, it is unlikely that a sedentary lifestyle will improve your cardiac status.

Prudent exercise, on the other hand, can prevent heart disease, and in most cases it will dramatically improve an already diseased or damaged heart. So what do we mean by prudent exercise? First of all, it must be designed for you specifically. This means you should get the supervision and approval of your physician; practice careful adherence to the prescribed program, and consider all the points covered in the following pages. It is strongly recommended that you take this book with you when you discuss your mending-heart fitness program with your medical advisor so there will be no misunderstanding of what is intended by either of you.

The exercise you need to improve your heart is aerobic exercise. You should exercise hard enough that it causes you to breathe deeply and increases your pulse rate to your ideal exercise pulse rate for a prolonged period of time—eventually forty-five minutes to one hour per day. As we have said before, the purpose of an aerobic exercise program is to build cardiovascular and cardiopulmonary strength and endurance—in other words, to strengthen your heart, lungs and circulatory system so they will function most efficiently and have adequate reserve in distressful and emergency situations. Most heart disease patients should be able to adopt this program with minimal difficulty and in a short time resume the most active, productive, confident, healthy, and happy life they have ever known.

You needn't walk more than four miles a day, and in some cases, not even that far. The time you spend walking is far more important than the actual distance. Set your sights on eventually walking one hour a day. Think you can't do an hour a day? Well, if you don't have a physically crippling disease or injury that keeps you from walking, you can probably walk an hour a day very easily if you build up to it. It is probably not a matter of physical inability but a matter of priority. Believe me, your health is well worth an hour a day. Busier people than you have found the time—so can you. And you must if you want to reach your full life potential.

My mother-in-law, at age eighty-three, had open heart surgery to replace a defective heart valve. In addition, she had a cardiac pacemaker installed. For at least two decades before her surgery she hadn't walked more than 100 feet at a time without sitting down for a prolonged rest. Within two days of her surgery we started her on a walking program. It started with a walk from her bed to the bathroom less than ten feet away. The next day, we walked her out into the hall a few feet, to a chair, and then back to her bed. She did that four times that day, and it exhausted her. The next day, we walked her in the hospital hall for about fifty feet and back to the chair, and after a brief rest she took another fifty foot walk and went back to bed. We did that routine about six times that day. The next day she walked about 100 feet of hallway about ten different times. She was surprised to discover that it was about a fifth of a mile.

Her walks increased daily, and by the time she left the hospital ten days after surgery, she was doing about a mile a day in the halls of the hospital in divided doses. She left the hospital about five days earlier than her surgeon expected her to, and he credited her rapid recovery to her daily walks.

When she got home, she started walking outside or in shopping centers when the weather was bad. Within four weeks of her hospital discharge, she was walking an hour nonstop and clipping off three miles, or a mile every twenty minutes. That's a comfortable and easy pace for most people. Today she walks a mile in sixteen to seventeen minutes with surprising ease for a ninety-year-old. She walks four miles a day six or seven days a week with a proud bounce to her stride. When the weather is good, she even plays nine holes of golf a week with the girls. She is healthier and more active than she's been in the past thirty years. Set your goals in her footsteps!

Discuss your walking plans with your personal medical advisor. Show her this book and decide at what level you should begin—and then begin today! If it's from your bed to the toilet and back, so be it. If you can walk a few hundred feet in the hall, so be it. If you can walk a mile, however slow, great! Wherever you can start, start—but start today!

Let's review all you have to gain:

- You will feel better all over, with fewer aches and pains. When something does bother you, you'll bounce back quicker.

- You'll look better and have more muscle tone throughout your entire body. You may not lose much weight, but you'll have less fat and look trimmer.

- You'll be happier, more confident, and have more energy and interests.

- You'll sleep better.

- You'll find your joints are more supple and limber and less subject to pain, injury, and stiffness.

- You'll think better, clearer, and more creatively because of the improved circulation to your brain.

- You'll want to get out and do things you thought you'd never be interested in again.

- You'll enjoy friends and relatives a lot more, and they'll enjoy you.

- You'll stop feeling sorry for yourself and may well want to help others achieve your state of health and happiness for themselves.

- You'll start looking for and setting new goals for yourself.

- You'll start thinking of your bright future instead of living in the past, realizing that your life is still very much in front of you.

So get up right now and take your first steps toward that new life in front of you!

FIVE

Simple Strategies for Sensible Eating

It is amazing that the tremendous increase in nutritional knowledge our scientists have accumulated in the past decade has supported the correctness of the diets our long-lived primitive counterparts have been eating for centuries. Some live worlds apart, but there are dramatic similarities in their diets that emphasize the importance of the foods we eat in determining our health. These peoples' diets have not come about due to insight or wisdom, but because of what has been provided for them by nature and tradition. Still, the effects are the same. They live long, healthy, active lives.

Further evidence of food's impact on our health can be found in the example of Japanese diets. Until Japanese diets were transformed by Western influence after World War II, Japanese people didn't have the same rates of heart problems, cancers, strokes, diabetes, or other terminal diseases that we have. Since their diets changed to emulate ours and since we began exporting our smoking habits to them, their death rates from these illnesses have skyrocketed to our levels—proof that our eating and smoking habits are killers.

Now that you've started an exercise program to put your cardiovascular system into better aerobic fitness, you should start to bring your nutrition into a life-preserving mode. Not only will the foods you eat from now on lengthen your life, but they will help keep you fit, give you energy for activity, and reduce many of the joint and muscle problems that put too many of us into rocking chairs and wheelchairs when we grow old.

The focus of your diet should be on nutrition and eating healthy, not necessarily on losing weight. If you happen to be one of those five percent who can take it off and keep it off, go for it. But if your weight has been yo-yoing up and down for the past decade or two, it's time to try a new approach. Folks who are destined to be heavy can still be healthy. Weight is only one factor in our total health profile, and if you can get the other factors in line, your weight need make little difference.

Let me also emphasize that dieting to lose weight rarely works. Oh, you may knock off twenty or thirty pounds on one diet or another, but as soon as you go off of it, you'll gain back twenty-five or thirty-five pounds— much more weight than you originally lost. Sound familiar? It should. National averages show that less than ten percent of us ever keep off the weight we lose with all the various diets we try from time to time. The yo-yoing of our weight during and between diets is much more unhealthy than the weight we originally wanted to take off. The focus of your eating habits should be maximizing your health, not minimizing your weight.

This book does not put you on a diet. In fact, if you follow this program you'll never diet again, and a year from today you'll be the healthiest you can be—possibly the healthiest you have ever been! That's the goal of this program: to put you into the best condition you can be in, to catapult you into the second half of your life, and to help you live as many healthy, productive, and pleasurable years of your 120-year potential as possible.

The first step toward eating to stay healthy rather than eating to lose weight is to accept that some of us, perhaps most of us, are just not destined to be the gods and goddesses we see in advertisements or to match a predetermined spot on a weight chart. Neither the weight charts nor the advertising industry is necessarily the best health standard for us to set our goals by. And just because we don't measure up—or rather down—to those arbitrary standards, does not mean we are any less valuable or less healthy than the skinnier folks.

This program will help you to set new, proper, healthy, realistic, and above all safe weight standards for yourself. Forget weight charts: they were invented by insurance companies, not public health authorities or physicians. Instead, you will learn in the next few chapters how to determine your own ideal body weight. It makes a lot more sense to establish and maintain a weight that fits you personally than to try to whittle yourself down to match the numbers on a chart. It is far more realistic, and it encourages healthier eating habits by making fad diets a thing of the past. In the last decade alone there have been hundreds, perhaps thousands of diet books published, and yet our population is probably more out of shape, obese, and unhealthy than ever before. This program will propose no new fad diet: we will discuss only good nutrition. You'll probably be surprised to discover that most overweight people are also malnourished. Correcting this malnourishment will do far more to improve your health than trying to shed extra pounds by starving yourself.

The ultimate goal should be good nutrition for a long, active, healthy life. It is pointless to spend your life trying to lose weight if you're not going to be healthy enough to enjoy it because of fad dieting and poor nutrition. So let's set your first goal at living as many of your potential 120 years as humanly possible and enjoying them all to their fullest.

Let's summarize:

1. You are never going to diet again. For us the word *diet* no longer exists. If we have to refer to it again, it will be reduced to *d—t.*

2. You are going to get as near your individual ideal body weight as you can and maintain it for life, whether that ideal body weight is higher or lower than your present weight.

3. In addition to being in control of your ideal body weight, a year from now you will be in the best health you can possibly attain.

Since we no longer recognize the word *d—t* we need a new concept—not a synonym, but a concept with truly a different meaning. It's not a coined concept or new idea. It's a concept you've known since at least grade school. But we'll personalize it for you, make it palatable to you, make it work for you, make it easily understood by you. You are the person who is the subject of this program. For it to succeed it has to succeed for you. The concept that will work for the rest of your life to help you achieve and maintain *your* ideal body weight is simple good nutrition.

The key word is *simple.* You needn't become a nutritionist. A few simple insights will let you select the best foods to satisfy your personal nutritional and appetite needs.

Defensive Shopping

Most advice about eating nutritiously comes in the form of lists: Eat these foods, don't eat those. Let's attack this problem a little differently. Our Third World friends don't live longer and eat better than we do because they're smarter than we are. They eat the way they do because nature has dealt them a kind hand. She's made the bad nutrition unavailable to them and put only healthy things in their food sources. So take a lesson from nature. Instead of listing all the things you should and shouldn't eat, try to make the bad stuff unavailable. If it's not there, you can't eat it. Thus, we should concentrate on *defensive shopping*. If you don't buy it, it won't be in your cupboard, and if it's not in the cupboard, you're not likely to eat it too often.

There are many things that influence our food selection when we shop. Recognizing them will help us to avoid stocking up on the wrong foods.

Tradition

Among the strongest selection forces as we shop are our ethnic backgrounds and family or cultural traditions. Nostalgia is a big factor in our shopping and eating habits. Just remembering my grandmother's apple strudel makes it difficult to pass up the pastry department without buying a desert that isn't going to help me reach my nutritional goals one bit. And even though there aren't too many bakeries that make a thin crust strudel like grandma did, the memory translates into apple turnovers, apple pie, apple tarts, apple Danish or anything else that smells and tastes of apples, cinnamon, nuts, raisins, and butter. And if I can't find something to satisfy that craving, there's always the great cheese cake my mom used to make!

Being of European and Jewish extraction, there are plenty of other things to whet my already too-easily-influenced appetite. Matzo ball soup, chopped liver, Polish sausage, corned beef, hot pastrami, Vienna pastries, Kaiser rolls, Hungarian pastries, herring in sour cream, cheeses, salami, sausages of all kinds, dumplings, goose—the list goes on and on. It's hard to walk through a market without remembering those delicacies and then buying everything in sight.

But there are also other fond memories: beet borscht, gefilte fish, roast chicken and turkey, good rye bread, lean boiled chicken or beef, baked fished, poached fish, smoked fish, all kinds of stews, hot vegetable soup, rice pudding. That list is also extensive, but it is a bit healthier than the first.

I can eat wonderful things that remind me of my childhood without paying for it on the scale. But I don't have to totally give up the items on the first list. Instead, I can fill my shopping cart from list two when I do everyday shopping and save the occasional item from list one for special occasions. They become that much more pleasant if they aren't an everyday event. A once-in-a-while delicatessen lunch out becomes a heavenly experience.

I've listed the items that turn my appetite on, and you'll have your own lists. The idea is for you to divide the foods into the same two categories I did: foods that are okay to have in your home on a regular basis and things to keep out except for infrequent special occasions. After you learn how to select healthy foods to keep in your home, you'll find there are still plenty of items to let you keep up the family, cultural, and ethnic traditions your stomach has become fond of.

Marketing

Next to what you like, the second strongest motivator of your buying habits is what your food market wants you to buy. There is a science and art to the way foods are displayed in the supermarkets. That art and science is aimed at only one thing: getting you to buy, buy, buy. It is not the intent of advertisers and marketers to make you buy things that are good for you; they want you to buy anything that's good for the supermarket's profit column. That's why when we go shopping, we invariably buy many items we had no intention of getting. How often have you gone into a store to pick up one ingredient you needed, say a dozen eggs, and come home with more than twenty dollars' worth of food you really didn't need? It was the result of good marketing.

Economic Status

Our economic status has a lot to do with how we buy food. If you don't think so, go into a supermarket in a part of town that is of a lower or higher economic status than where you live or usually shop. You'll be amazed at how even the same food chains will stock their stores differently in other areas of town. And as you might expect, the prices on the same items will vary from area to area. The most significant fact in all this is that as economic status increases, the food we eat tends to become less healthy. You won't easily find prime beef in poorer neighborhoods, and prime beef is much higher in fat and cholesterol than U.S. Good or Choice meats. Poorer areas will sell more chicken, beans, and inexpensive fish. The fancier neighborhood stores will sell more expensive seafoods like lobster, shrimp, crab, and shellfish, all of which are more unhealthy than the cheaper fish. Part of the reason many people in the Third World eat healthier than we do is that they can't afford many of the exotic foods that are less healthy. Again, I'm not suggesting you never eat a lobster, crab, shrimp, or oyster again, but I am suggesting you keep those foods for special occasions and eat the healthier foods on a more regular basis. And there are plenty of healthy exotic foods you'll love.

Convenience is another unhealthy trend that the rich can better afford. Today the markets are full of already-prepared dinners and dishes. Read the labels on those foods, and you'll see they are usually high in fats, salt, preservatives, and other chemicals that are not good for us. Nothing beats fresh foods prepared in your own kitchen where you can control all that goes into them.

Habits

Our eating patterns and thus our buying patterns are largely dictated by habit. Some of our eating habits are good. Some are bad. All you need to do is learn which habits are good and emphasize them. Then add a few more good habits you can learn to love and de-emphasize the bad ones, completely eliminating those you can learn to live without. Our eating habits determine what we buy. But the easiest way to change our eating habits is to change our buying habits. As I said before, "If it's not in the cupboard, it will be tough for you to eat it!" From now on, stock up your cupboards with good, tasty, fun, and enjoyable food that also happens to be nutritious and healthy. That's what I mean by defensive shopping.

Just what do our long-lived Third World cousins eat? Actually their health comes only partly from what they eat. Just as important is what they don't eat. Because of their environment and economic circumstances, they eat very little red meat, and what little red meat they do eat is usually very lean. Our Third World counterparts usually live on islands, in the jungle, or high in mountains where grazing is impractical or where red meat is just too costly for their meager incomes. Whatever the reason, they get most of their meat protein from chicken and fish. Their red meat consumption is from the rare lamb, goat, or pig slaughtered for very special celebrations. This translates into very low animal-fat consumption and low cholesterol in their diets.

In addition to their low animal-fat consumption, people from primitive areas of the world tend to eat foods high in fiber. Fruits and vegetables are a major part of their readily available provisions. They can often be homegrown on small plots and require no refrigeration. They can be stored without high-tech methods. Many fruits grow wild and are available for the picking. These people do not have the equipment or the economy to afford the refining of grains. So, they use whole-grain wheat, rice, oats, maize, and whichever other grains are available. They eat their fruits and vegetables raw or only slightly cooked so the fiber is not broken down in preparation. All these factors increase the roughage or fiber in their daily food consumption.

Their consumption of dairy products and eggs is also minimized, not because they are wiser than we are, but because of their economic situation. They eat relatively few eggs because it is more prudent to sell eggs or let them hatch into edible poultry. The goat milk that they get from their herds is better used in the production of cheeses, which they can sell to wealthier people. These factors also reduce the animal fat and cholesterol in their diets.

What is the overall effect of these factors? Reduction of dietary animal fat translates into reduction of heart disease, hypertension, and stroke. Increase of fiber consumption translates into reduction of cancer, blood sugar levels, arteriosclerosis, and many other chronic health problems that plague our society. In fact, the diseases that are responsible for most of the deaths in the United States—

heart disease, cancer, stroke, hypertension, diabetes, kidney failure—are not frequently found in primitive areas of the world. Nutrition is probably the major factor in this difference. Relatively simple changes in our nutrition could reduce—and perhaps help us to eliminate—these diseases from our society. Certainly if you make these changes in your own nutrition, you'll be reducing your chances of developing these dread diseases. Reduce the chances of developing the diseases that kill most Americans and you'll be taking a long stride toward increasing your longevity to that 120-year potential of active, quality life.

Making Changes

Now that we've pointed out the trouble spots, the next step is to start making some painless changes and begin building a diet full of nutritious and enjoyable foods. You don't have to deny yourself delicious meals or tasty snacks to be healthy. There are good-for-you substitutions for almost every unhealthy ingredient. Below is a list of foods that you should try to avoid and a list of foods that can be substituted for each unhealthy item.

Dairy Products

Avoid	Substitute
Whole milk	Skim milk
	Butter milk
	1% milk (has more fat than is good)
	Powdered milk
Coffee cream	Non-dairy creamer
Butter	Olive oil (flavored if you like)
Margarine	Olive oil
	Fruit spread

Simple Strategies for Sensible Eating

Avoid	Substitute
Ice cream	Sherbets
	Ice milk
	Low-fat, low-cal frozen dessert
	Fat free frozen yogurt
	Non-dairy frozen desserts
High-fat cheeses	Low-fat cheeses

Snacks

Avoid	Substitute
Potato chips	Popcorn and pretzels
Candy	Dietetic candy
Cookies	Fruits
Crackers and munchies	Raw vegetables

Breads

Avoid	Substitute
White breads and rolls	Whole-wheat breads and rolls
White soda crackers	Whole-grain crackers
Cereals	High-fiber cereals

Meats

Avoid	Substitute
Red meats	Poultry:
Beef	Turkey
Pork	Chicken
Lamb	Fish
Veal	Buffalo
	Duck*
	Goose*
Egg	Non-cholesterol egg substitutes

*Duck and Goose, though high in fat, are not really bad for you because they are extremely high in monounsaturated fat. At room temperature their fats (*schmaltz*) are liquid and they are almost as good for you as olive oil. But watch out for the calories. If you skin duck and goose before cooking, they are a healthy substitute for other meats high in saturated fats.

This is but a brief listing of the things you should avoid and a few of their substitutes. It does not mean you can never eat things from the first column. But the less you stock the unhealthy items, the easier and sooner you'll get them out of your eating-habit system. Eliminating these most common less healthy foods is a good start on the road to good nutrition. Later, you'll learn how to select the best foods for you and your family, and you'll begin to really rid yourself of harmful items.

The idea is that once you discover how to detect foods that are unhealthy for you and your family, you'll avoid them. Don't let them be easily available for frequent consumption. Don't let them back into your home except on special and rare occasions. Don't let them back into your habit system. It's not that difficult to find healthier treats to replace them.

SIX

Labels: Don't Believe Everything You Read

In December 1992, food labeling laws were dramatically changed and supposedly toughened for the protection of the consumer. That is true to a degree, but in some ways they became a bit more confusing, leaving plenty of room for manufacturers to mislead the unwary. In this brief chapter, I hope to make the unwary aware!

First, let's look at some of the positive features of the labeling laws as they stand today. Before the new regulations became law, manufacturers used terms like *healthy*, *light*, *reduced*, *free*, or almost any other term at their own discretion. Now these terms have been defined, and a manufacturer using the expressions on a label must meet certain FDA standards. Furthermore, food advertisements have to follow the same guidelines. Today, if a manufacturer uses the term *low*, as in "low fat," the product must have no more than three grams of fat per serving. A product claiming to be "low in saturated fat" must have one gram or less of saturated fat per serving and can have no more than fifteen percent of all its calories from saturated fat. A "low calorie" product can have no more than forty calories per serving.

Perhaps the most significant factor in the present law is that the government now defines *serving*. Previously, manufacturers claimed a serving to be ridiculously small so they could claim minimal calories per serving. For example, a serving was smaller than a single square of chocolate, or three potato chips, or a single small cookie. Today, servings are more realistically defined as how much the average person actually eats at a sitting. This forces manufacturers to state more realistic figures for calories per serving.

If a manufacturer claims his product to be "high" in a nutrient, as in "high fiber," that product must have at least twenty percent or more of that nutrient's daily minimum requirement. *Light* means the product has no more than half the fat or one-third the calories of its "regular" counterpart. Make sure that when you see the word *light* on a package that the manufacturer is not referring to "light taste" in smaller type. The term can still be used to describe taste, texture, or color. The term *reduced* cannot be used unless the product has twenty-five percent less of reduced ingredient.

Free means free of a substance normally found in the product, or that the substance is in an insignificant quantity in a single serving. This is one area in which you can be easily deceived. If a product has less than one gram of fat per serving, the manufacturer can claim it to be "fat free." Now, if one serving, say two cookies, has 0.9 grams, and you eat eight cookies, you would be getting 3.6 grams of fat from your "fat-free" cookies. Multiply that by nine (the number of calories in one gram of fat) and you'll be getting 32.4 calories of fat, probably all saturated, from your "fat-free" snack.

Labels: Don't Believe Everything You Read

To use the term *healthy* on a package or advertisement, the product has to meet the definitions of "low fat and saturated fat" and "limited sodium and cholesterol," plus have at least ten percent of the daily requirement of at least one of the following nutrients in naturally occurring forms: vitamins A or C, iron, calcium, protein, or fiber.

Now, let's look at a typical food label. This label is from the side of a Nabisco Ginger Snaps box. In bold letters at the top, the label claims that there is "no cholesterol" in the product and only "low saturated fat." By the new definitions, this means that there is no dietary cholesterol such as that found in eggs, dairy products, or meats. But remember, dietary cholesterol is not as dangerous as saturated fat when it comes to raising your LDL (bad cholesterol). The manufacturer can claim "low saturated fat" because there are less than three grams of saturated fat in one serving, which the label states as being four cookies— about 28 grams.

Everything that is defined on the rest of the label is based on a four-cookie serving. If you eat more than four, you must interpolate by increasing the numbers by twenty-five percent for each added cookie you eat. The number of calories derived from a four-cookie serving is 120. If you ate five cookies, you would have to increase that total by twenty-five percent, or thirty calories. The number of calories in five cookies, then, is 120 plus 30, or 150 calories. The label also states that twenty-five of the 120 calories in a serving come from fat.

You must also use caution when considering the "percent daily value" figures for fat, cholesterol, sodium, carbohydrates, fiber, and protein. Note first that an asterisk points out that this information is based on a two-thousand-calorie-per-day diet. In other words, if you eat fewer than two thousand calories a day, the percentages given will be too low for you, and if you eat more than two thousand calories a day, the percentages will be too high. But also be careful not to confuse "percent daily value" with the percentage of a substance found in the product as a whole.

This can be tricky, and the manufacturers love it. For example, when the phrase, "Total Fat: 2.5g . . . 4%," appears on the label as a "percent daily value," too many customers are led to think, "Only four percent fat—great!" After all, the American Heart Association says to limit yourself to foods that have less than thirty percent of their calories from fat. You must remember, however, that this figure represents a "percent of daily value." This means that the amount of fat in this serving of four cookies is four percent of all the fat calories you are allowed in a full day if you normally consume two thousand calories per day. It does *not* mean that only four percent of the calories in that serving are from fat. The percentage of fat calories in this serving is found by multiplying the number of fat grams per serving (2.5) by the number of calories per gram of fat (9), which comes to 22.5 calories from fat per serving. 22.5 is about twenty percent of 120 (the number of total calories per serving), so about twenty percent of the total calories per serving is from fat. Now in this case, that's okay, but too often a product with well over forty percent fat calories gets mistaken for one with only "ten percent fat" (the daily allowance)!

Probably the most important information a label can convey—even more than how *much* fat—is the breakdown of *what kinds* of fat we're getting from a product. In this case, we're getting all saturated fat, the worst kind. As you will see in the next chapter, saturated fat is the kind that raises your LDL cholesterol, the bad cholesterol. It is even worse than dietary cholesterol itself. Furthermore, this

Labels: Don't Believe Everything You Read

product gives you no monounsaturated fat, which raises your HDL cholesterol, the good cholesterol..

The next percent daily value listed is for dietary cholesterol: zero percent. No dietary cholesterol does not mean a product is safe, although that is what manufacturers want you to believe. A product with no dietary cholesterol but a high level of saturated fat will do you more harm than a product with some dietary cholesterol and low saturated fat—especially if the second product has a relatively high percentage of monounsaturated fat. Again, we'll discuss the signifcance of the different kinds of fats further in the next chapter.

The remaining percent daily values are for fiber, sugars, protein, and carbohydrates. Of these, fiber is perhaps most important; the higher the fiber content of a food, the better. As you compare fat grams to protein and carbohydrate grams, remember that every gram of protein and carbohydrate represents four calories, and every gram of fat is nine calories—more than twice as many. Manufacturers must also list the amount of iron, calcium, and vitamins A and C that a product has. They can also choose to list other nutrients, but are not required to do so.

Another mandatory part of every label that is worth reading is the list of ingredients. The ingredients are listed in order of their quantity in the product. On this label, enriched flour is first, meaning it is the ingredient found in greatest quantity. It is good to note that sugar is rather far down the list in this product. Note that the shortening used is a vegetable oil, which is good, but that it has been partially hydrogenated. This is not so good, because as we will discuss in the next chapter, hydrogenation destroys the benefits of unsaturated fats. It is also important to read the list of ingredients if you or someone who will be eating the product has allergies.

Make yourself become a label reader. Between this information and what you will learn from the next chapter and glossary, you need no longer be at the mercy of unscrupulous manufacturers and their Madison Avenue marketing geniuses!

SEVEN

In Defense of Fat

Now that you're approaching or entering your second half of life, you may be pleased to hear that a pinch of fat under the skin isn't as bad as it used to be. Of course, vanity may try to tell you otherwise, but as far as your health is concerned, you can actually handle a little gain. Now that doesn't mean that you can simply let yourself go, but as we grow older, one of the bonuses is that we can tolerate a little higher fat-to-lean ratio.

In fact, fat on the whole doesn't entirely deserve the bad reputation it's gotten. I'm not here to tell you that fat is all good on you or for you. Far from it! But it isn't all bad either. God didn't put fat on us just to be mean or have a good laugh. Fat has a purpose, and it is essential to life.

We can see the purpose of fat a little more easily when we look at its function on lower animals. Because of our adopted lifestyle, some of these needs and purposes for fat have become less obvious and important. However, we still don't differ too much from animals in the wild to require the benefits of *some* fat.

Purposes of Fat

Retention of Heat

Bears, otters, seals, whales, and almost all other animals, including humans, are insulated against cold weather by our subdermal layer of fat. Because of the garment industry, this insulating layer of fat is not as important to us as it was to our cave-dwelling ancestors. However, it can still be a lifesaving insulator under extreme conditions. It increases our survival time in cold water, extremely frigid weather, or other forms of unexpected exposure. We heavier folks usually tolerate cold weather better because our bodies conserve heat better than our thinner friends.

Storage of Energy

Hibernating animals or animals that may be forced to fast for long periods between kills, rely upon their fat stores for energy. Because humans no longer depend on successful hunting, fat storage for long fasts is not often important, but as an energy source, fat still plays a major role. The problem most of us have is that we deposit more storage fat than we burn off. Thus, exercise is important to any weight or fat reduction/control program. Our bodies are marvels of efficiency and can get by on much less food energy than most of us tend to consume. The balance goes to fat storage deposits.

Raw Materials for Hormones and Body Functions

If our bodies were devoid of fat, we could not produce hormones that are vital to life and reproduction. Additionally, there are fat soluble essential vitamins, body oils, enzymes, digestive fluids, and brain and central nervous system tissues that rely on fats for their function, regeneration, production, and maintenance.

Body Contour

Subdermal fat deposits, when properly distributed, give our bodies—especially female bodies—those attractive curves that are so much desired. Sadly, all too often, these deposits are not distributed the way we want them to be. Furthermore, this distribution is usually hereditary. Spot exercising, which has been so popular as a tool to reshape the body, does not work for the majority of us. Still, it is important to remember that the way our fat is distributed is not the problem. Rather, it is the amount of *excess* fat on our bodies. Even if exercising does not redistribute your fat to give you the sculpted contours you might like, it helps burn excess fat from your body, which is what's important from the perspective of your health.

Flotation

Because fat is less dense than water, it adds to buoyancy. This is of great importance to swimming animals, less important to us humans. In fact, when I scuba dive it becomes a problem, and I have to wear a few pounds (actually more than a few pounds) of lead to help me get under.

Skin Oils

Oils are the liquid form of fat and thus, our body oils are fats. These are of great importance in maintaining healthy skin and hair. Oils protect us from environmental assaults such as air, water, sun, heat, and cold.

Trauma Protection

There are areas of fat around many of our vital organs that protect them from trauma. Just as styrofoam packing insulates and protects precious and fragile objects from damaging impacts when shipped, so body fat reduces the chances of damage to delicate organs from blunt trauma.

Manufacture of Good Cholesterol

What is "good cholesterol"? Isn't cholesterol what everyone has been telling us to avoid these last ten years? Well, all cholesterol isn't bad. However, the bad cholesterol, *low-density lipid* or *LDL*, is very bad. It causes atherosclerosis or fatty deposits in blood vessels all over the body, including in your brain and your heart, disrupting circulation, causing strokes, and precipitating myocardial infarctions or heart attacks. LDL cholesterol also is implicated as a causative agent in numerous cancers. LDL is a very bad character and should be avoided. Avoidance is best accomplished by reducing your consumption of saturated fats. *High-density lipid*, or *HDL*, cholesterol is a good guy! HDL cholesterol protects you from harmful LDL cholesterol. HDL cholesterol is actually desirable to have on board. It binds up LDL and prevents it from damaging your body, protecting you against myocardial infarction, stroke, and several types of cancers. Therefore, it is desirable to have a good HDL-to-LDL ratio circulating in your blood. The way to raise your HDL while lowering your LDL is to limit your fat consumption to monounsaturated fats as much as possible. Also, exercise will raise your HDL cholesterol while lowering your LDL.

These are but a few of the more important functions of body fat. A totally fat free diet would be a serious detriment to our well-being. Indeed, we could not long survive eating no fat. This does not mean I advocate total abandon when it comes to ingesting and storing fat. But it may be better for you to carry a little excess fat than to maintain a deficit in body fat. Fat is not all bad, as advertisers would have you think. Some fats are very beneficial to our health!

Let's take a closer look at how much fat we should carry on our bodies and what kinds of fats are safest for us to ingest. We don't want to eliminate fat from our nutrition, but rather to exchange an acceptable quantity of healthy types of fats and oils for an unacceptable quantity of those fats and oils known to be detrimental to our health and longevity.

Fats and Oils: Healthy vs. Harmful

Let's review the definition of "fat" as it appears in the glossary at the end of this book. "Fat: an essential nutrient of plant or animal origin. Only about one tablespoon of unsaturated fat is needed daily for good nutrition. Fat supplies nine calories of energy per gram making it twice as fattening as carbohydrate and protein when ingested in excess."

An average person requires about fifteen calories per day to maintain each pound of his body weight. That means a 150-pound person requires about 150 times fifteen calories, or 2,250 calories per day to maintain his weight. A one hundred-pound person would require 1,500 daily calories and a two hundred-pound person could eat three thousand calories without altering his body weight. According to the American Heart Association, a person should acquire less than one third of those calories from fats. I personally feel you should try to hold that closer to ten or twenty percent of your daily calories from fat, and those should be from monounsaturated fats, which lower LDL and raise HDL.

Fats can be divided into *saturated* and *unsaturated*. Saturated fats, like those in butter and lard, are most often derived from animal and dairy foods and are usually hard at room temperatures. Saturated fats tend to raise cholesterol levels in blood and should be considered unhealthy. Coconut oil and palm oil are vegetable fats that have similar properties to saturated animal fats. They too should be avoided.

COMPARISON OF DIETARY FATS IN ORDER OF THEIR HEALTHFULNESS:

DIETARY FAT SOURCE	% CHOLESTEROL (mg/tbs)	% SATURATED	% UNSATURATED (% poly.) (%mono.)	
Canola oil	0	6	32	62
Olive oil	0	14	9	77
Safflower oil	0	10	77	13
Sunflower oil	0	11	69	20
Corn oil	0	13	62	25
Soybean oil	0	15	61	24
Peanut oil	0	18	33	49
Cottonseed oil	0	25	50	25
Lard	12	41	12	47
Beef tallow	14	52	4	44
Butter fat	33	66	4	30
Palm oil	0	83	2	15
Coconut oil	0	92	2	6

From the USDA Agricultural Handbook 8-4, *1979.*

This table shows different dietary fats in decreasing order of healthfulness to humans. Canola oil is healthiest and coconut oil is least healthy. Determination of healthfulness in this case is measured as how much a particular fat or oil will tend to raise your blood cholesterol level. You will notice that even though palm oil and coconut oil are vegetable fats and contain no cholesterol, their levels of saturated fat are so high that they are less healthy for you than the listed animal fats. This shows you that just because a product boasts "no cholesterol," it is not necessarily good for you. You must learn to read ingredient labels to get the whole story and avoid those products rich in saturated fats. Also, you must learn to limit your ingestion of the good fats. Remember, the body needs only about two or three teaspoons of fat per day; any more than that is excessive.

Latest studies show that monounsaturated fats are actually good for you, in that they lower your LDL and raise your HDL. The highest monounsaturated fats are canola, olive, and fish oils. Goose and duck grease (schmaltz) are also high in monounsaturated fat, but don't forget the calories!

Recent studies also show that dietary cholesterol does not necessarily raise your blood cholesterol. Our bodies actually use the saturated fats we ingest to make the cholesterol that circulates in our blood. Additionally, for the most part, our bodies break down and excrete the cholesterol we eat. In other words, the saturated fat in a food is more harmful than the actual cholesterol in a food. This being the case, eggs are not nearly as bad for you as was originally thought, because although they are high in dietary cholesterol, they are also high in monounsaturated fat and lecithin, both of which raise HDL (the good guys) and lower LDL (the bad guys).

Unsaturated fats, which can be polyunsaturated or monounsaturated, are liquid at room temperature (oils) and are usually vegetable in origin. Fish oils are examples of oils derived from animals. They tend to lower blood cholesterol. Some vegetable oils, such as margarine, have been treated chemically (hydrogenated) to solidify them at room temperature. Hydrogenation diminishes the health benefits of unsaturated fats.

How Much Fat Is Right for You?

Fat does not necessarily cause death. Fat, however, is all too often a symptom of those factors that do cause untimely deaths. Too often, fat people lead sedentary lifestyles. Such habits tend to increase one's chances for an early death. If a person with some excess fat is also active in aerobic activities, she may well have a healthy body capable of sustaining long life.

A fat person might be heavy because she eats too much of the wrong foods and has high cholesterol with low HDL and high LDL. High cholesterol with low HDL and high LDL greatly increases one's chances for an early demise. On the other hand, a person might have a hereditary predisposition for being overweight even though she eats nourishing foods and maintains a low total cholesterol with a relatively high HDL and low LDL. That person is not necessarily at higher risk of early death because of her higher body fat ratio.

Often, folks who are under a great deal of stress tend to overeat as a defense mechanism. This can lead to excess fat deposits. The distress is the potential killer, and the fat may be only a less lethal symptom of the distress. Another person who might be somewhat overweight with a little excessive fat-to-lean mass ratio, but who is relatively happy with her lot, may be at no great risk of early death or serious illness. Again, this is not to say that excessive fat can't be a detriment to good health, but a moderate amount of body fat may well be better for you than constantly trying to attain an unrealistic weight goal.

So, how much fat is acceptable? Let's consider body fat in terms of heart attack risk. The following table indicates heart attack risks as: very low, low, moderate, high, and very high and correlates them with varying body fat percentages in men and women:

In Defense of Fat

HEART ATTACK RISK FACTOR FOR VARIOUS BODY FAT PERCENTAGES

	VERY LOW	LOW	MODERATE	HIGH	VERY HIGH
Women	15%	20%	25%	33%	40%+
Men	12%	16%	22%	25%	30%+

Remember that these risks are affected by other factors. If you smoke, are under great stress, eat foods that are poor in nutrition, have high blood pressure, are diabetic, do not exercise regularly in a vigorous aerobic program, and/or have a family history of heart disease, you may be pushed into a high risk category even though your body fat may be in only the low to moderate range.

Age also affects acceptable body fat percentages. As we get older we can carry a little more fat and still consider ourselves fit—to a point. The following tables show how age affects permissible body fat percentages among men and women:

MAXIMUM BODY FAT PERCENTAGES FOR GOOD FITNESS

AGE	20-29	30-39	40-49	50-59	60+
Men	20%	22%	24%	26%	27%
Women	24%	26%	27%	29%	30%

It's important to remember that these figures represent *maximum* percentages. In general, health status increases as body fat percentage decreases. A fifty-year-old man—whatever his weight—can have up to twenty-six percent body fat and still feel comfortable with his health status. If he were to take steps to lower his body fat percentage, however, his health would still improve. You must also remember that body fat percentage is not a guaranteed indicator of your fitness level. Many other factors, such as inactivity, smoking, and poor nutrition, can be detrimental to overall fitness even in people with relatively low body fat. Body fat percentage is, however, a *much* more reliable indicator of health status than weight. Your ideal body weight will not be at a point on a weight chart, but rather somewhere near the best body fat percentage for your age and gender.

There are several ways to have your body fat percentage determined, but sad to say, none are as simple as stepping on a scale. Among them are the water immersion, caliper fat-fold measurement, electrical resistance, and infrared wand methods. Many doctors, health clubs and spas, hospitals, and clinics have the necessary equipment to measure your body fat percentage with at least one of these methods. The methods vary in accuracy and range in expense from free caliper measurements at health clubs to $150 for a water immersion test at a hospital. I believe that body fat percentage determination will become far more common in the near future, bringing down the cost of the procedure and greatly increasing the accuracy of the tests. Technology may even make an inexpensive, accurate, home testing procedure available in the near future.

Once you have determined your body fat percentage, you will have a choice to make. You can choose to bring it to a more acceptable level by increasing your muscle mass or by lowering your fat. More than likely you will choose a combination of the two. When you attain a body fat percentage and a fitness level that lets you feel your best, you will probably be near your own ideal body weight. That is a primary goal of this program.

But since we are not going to use weight as a major method of evaluating progress and fitness, we need other criteria for surveying improvement. Let's move on to the next step, which should help you set new and realistic goals for yourself—and provide more meaningful measures of your success.

EIGHT

Weights and Measures

If you're sick of stepping up on the scale and being frustrated with what you see, then this chapter is for you! Every d—t book you pick up is based on your losing pounds, pounds, and more pounds. When you go to a physician and she puts you on a d—t, she will probably gauge your progress, success, or failure, completely by your weight change. It is a premise of this program that weight is the least important measure of your success with turning your health around. There are a number of measures of your health status that are far more telling than your scale. We have been misled to believe that if we don't look like models or match a number on a weight chart then we are unacceptable and in terrible health. Let's look at these other, better measures of health.

Your Ideal Body Weight

We've mentioned the concept of ideal body weight before; let's examine it a bit more closely. Two people might be the same height and have the same bone structure. One might be of average stature, slim, and right on the button with his weight as recommended by the weight chart. The second fellow may be athletic, well-muscled, and broad-shouldered with full biceps and triceps, heavily muscled thighs and calves, and a hard, flat stomach. Because of his well-muscled body, he wears a coat two sizes larger than his slimmer counterpart. He may also wear a belt two inches smaller than the scrawny man because of his well-toned and flat abdomen. Because muscle tissue is relatively heavy compared to fatty tissue, our athletic friend may outweigh his more sedentary counterpart by twenty or thirty pounds. According to the weight chart, the more athletic person is "overweight," and by its standards, "unfit!" Our other friend, the less athletic, more sedentary of the two, is right on with the weight chart, implying that he is more "fit," healthier, and right where he should be to live a long healthy life. Right?

Wrong! Our athletic, well-muscled friend, although thirty or more pounds heavier, probably has far less body fat—in terms of both actual fat mass and body fat percentage—than his sedentary friend. And since the lighter of the two is sedentary, he has less energy, less endurance, less strength, less resistance to illness, less resistance to injury, and worst of all, he has far worse cardiovascular and cardiopulmonary health. Chances are, the thinner of our two friends has a higher blood pressure and a much higher resting pulse rate. Blood analysis will probably show his cholesterol to be higher with a low HDL (good cholesterol) and high LDL (bad cholesterol) when compared to his heavier counterpart. Ironically, the thinner of the two will have an easier time buying life and health insurance. Insurance companies like people to fit the charts.

The fact remains, however, that our heavier friend is much closer to, if not right on his ideal body weight, and although our thinner friend may be right on according to the weight chart, he may be under his ideal body weight.

Now let's say that Bill's heavy friend, call him Jack, convinces his thin but sedentary buddy, Bill, that he should get more active. They start to work out together. Bill isn't interested in building a muscular body like Jack's, but would like to firm up a little, develop more endurance, and especially strengthen his heart, lungs, and circulatory system.

Bill, being right on the spot as far as his weight chart states, does not feel he needs to d—t, but Jack shows him that he could eat more nutritiously by watching his fat and sugar consumption a little more closely and by adding some high-fiber foods to his daily consumption. Jack says nothing about the quantity of food Bill should eat, only the quality. They never discuss calories. Jack also gets Bill to join him in his daily aerobic workouts. Since Bill isn't interested in building a more muscular body, Jack doesn't involve Bill in the anaerobic bodybuilding workouts that he does three times a week in addition to his aerobics. Over the next few weeks, Bill has some surprises.

Weight Gain

Bill's biggest surprise was an initial weight gain. After all, he was watching his nutritional intake more closely, and although he wasn't on a d—t, he'd made every effort to reduce his fat consumption and had markedly increased his fiber intake. Why wouldn't that make him lose weight, especially since he was vigorously engaging in an aerobic exercise program?

The answer is simple! Fat weighs less than muscle! The reduction of fat and increased fiber consumption was beginning to melt away the body fat Bill did have, although there never was much there, and the calories he burned in his aerobic exercise helped to burn it off too. But the exercise did something more. It began to tone his muscles and actually put some muscle mass on his bones, especially in his legs, back, stomach, and shoulders. The net result was a slight weight gain. He was leaving his perfect perch on the weight chart and was moving toward his own ideal body weight. His percentage of body fat was reducing, muscle mass was increasing, and he was actually gaining weight—but it was healthy weight.

Had Bill just been following his weight as it pertained to a weight chart, as most people and physicians do when starting on a d—t, he would have considered his program a failure and a detriment to his health. Thus, he realized that weight was the least important measure of his physical condition. Bill began taking greater interest in other signs and measures of his successful progress.

Muscles Toned Up

Although Bill's exercise program raised his weight slightly, he soon stopped looking for increased fat deposits to account for it. He soon realized that he'd begun putting on some new muscle tissue. The flab was being replaced by stronger, well-toned muscle. In spite of his slight weight gain, Bill noticed that his clothing began to fit him loosely in places. It began to make sense that if fat weighed less than muscle, a pound of fat would take up more space than a pound of muscle. Thus, if he exchanged a pound of fat for a pound of muscle, the overall *size* of his body would actually diminish because muscle mass is more compact. Though weight went on, inches around the belt came off. His clothes began feeling a little tight in the chest and thighs and looser in the waist and hips. These were far better signs of his health than his position on a weight chart. Bill realized that it made more sense to measure body circumferences once a week than to weigh body mass daily. A simple tape measure could tell him more than his expensive new electronic state-of-the-art scale. He began taking weekly measurements around his waist, hips, chest, thighs, and neck.

Pulse Slowed

As the heart becomes stronger through aerobic exercise, it also becomes more efficient. Its stroke volume increases; more blood is pumped with each contraction. More oxygen gets to the muscles and organs of the body with less effort on the part of the heart. As a result, Bill's resting pulse went down because his now healthier heart didn't have to beat as often to supply his resting body with oxygen. By the same token, his heart didn't have to work as hard during activity to keep him going. The exercise that raised his pulse to 150 beats per minute when he first started working out now raised it only to 140 beats per minute. To get the same cardiopulmonary benefit, Bill had to increase his activity rate to bring his pulse back up to 150. His exercise pulse rate will continue to determine how hard he works out. A slowing pulse rate is one of the best indicators of cardiovascular/cardiopulmonary improvement.

Blood Pressure Fell

One of the best methods of bringing down blood pressure is to exercise. A one-hour-a-day, vigorous aerobic exercise program will do more to bring an elevated blood pressure down for most people than all the medications in the world. Reducing blood pressure is one of the best measures of your general fitness. As you approach your ideal body weight, your blood pressure should also approach an ideal level for you.

Distress Decreased

There is stress and distress. Stress is an important part of life. It is a motivator. It keeps us out of ruts. It makes us get up and do things. Stress is what made you get involved with this program. Something about your physical condition made you feel uneasy (stressful) enough to seek a solution to your less-than-satisfactory health status. Stress is good because it makes you dissatisfied with the status quo.

If, on the other hand, you do nothing about your dissatisfaction, or if you try to make changes and fail, stress becomes distress—and distress is not good. It is not stress that brings on heart attacks but the state of unresolved anger (distress) that results when your stress-motivated actions don't improve the stressing situation.

As Bill's physical health improved, he noticed a reduction in his distress and anger levels. Two factors contributed to this. First, exercise is one of the best reducers of distress and anger known to man. Exercise offers you an opportunity to "work off" hostility. As hostility and anger are reduced, distress is lowered. Second, as health status improves, you tend to attack your distressing problems with an energy and vigor that helps solve them before they have a chance to affect your health. When you notice that things just don't get to you the way they used to, you can be sure you're making real progress. It beats anything your scale can tell you about yourself! Also, exercise stimulates right-brain activity that helps to solve problems on a subconscious level. Often, at the end of a workout begun in a quandary, a solution to the problem will come to you like a sudden revelation. You may never even realize that your right brain, stimulated by the exercise, was busy solving your dilemma all the time.

Energy Increased

Activity breeds activity. As the percentage of body fat comes down and muscle tone, strength, and cardiovascular and cardiopulmonary efficiency increase, energy abounds. Most important, the desire to be sedentary begins to fade. A healthy body wants to be active. As his energy increased, Bill wanted more activity.

Productivity Increased

As Bill's health status improved and his energy level rose, problems began not to bother him as much as they did before—often because they seemed to get solved before they had a chance to bother him. His productivity level had risen dramatically. He got things done and found himself looking for more. Sitting on a couch and watching television just didn't cut it anymore. He began to seek out new interests and activities. He found fun in things that previously were chores, and he found more time for the things he used to enjoy but for which he never used to have the energy. When he began to notice that new fullness and fulfillment in his life, he can began to worry less about what his scale said.

Felt Terrific

Think about the way you've been feeling over the past few years. Try to remember what it's been like up to now, because as you get into your new lifestyle and health program you'll be amazed at how great you can feel when your health status turns around. Your new energy level, endurance, and interests will let you know in no uncertain terms that you are getting better every day—even if your weight stays the same or goes up a little.

Confidence Grew

When everything is getting better, you'll notice there's a new confidence about you in everything you attempt. As you begin to solve your problems, to find new energy to accomplish what you want, to feel better each day, to take on a better shape, you can't help but develop a newfound confidence in anything you want to do. Success begets success in everything you do.

Others Began to Comment Positively

Not only did Bill notice all these changes in himself, but others noticed too. He began to hear comments such as "You look like you're losing weight!" (even though he wasn't) and "What's different about you?" As you begin to reap the benefits of your new health program, you too will be able to measure your progress not by your weight but by the comments of others. Remarks such as "You're a new woman!" "You seem to have taken ten years off!" and, "I can't get over the changes in you!" will become familiar. Certainly they will make you feel better than the comments you've probably been hearing about yourself for the last few years.

Began to Enjoy Life

When life becomes more and more of a joy each day, you don't have to get on a scale to know you're improving your health status. When was the last time you couldn't wait for morning to come so you could attack life with a vengeance? That's what you should be looking forward to—not how much you gained or lost since yesterday.

Now if you want to weigh yourself for old time's sake, go ahead. Just remember that what you see on the scale has little to do with how you are or how you feel!

NINE

Keeping the Odds in Your Favor

In the beginning of this book I stated that the human body was designed to survive in good working order for at least 120 years. Obviously few of us are reaching that potential. We've malnourished ourselves, poisoned ourselves, misused ourselves, and let ourselves run down. Despite all that, 75,000 of us will be living to more than 100 years in just a half decade from now, and that number is increasing at a dizzying rate. This chapter will give you a few hints that, in addition to the aforementioned lifestyle changes, can help tip the odds in your favor. You want to do everything you can to be among those celebrating their one-century birthday—and enjoying the party!

As with the lifestyle changes we've discussed so far, some of the suggestions discussed here are prevention techniques. They keep you from doing damage to your body that can shorten its potential longevity. The rest are, for the most part, survival techniques, though some are also preventative. They increase the odds that you will survive dread illnesses should they befall you. Discuss them with your medical advisors if you have any question about their appropriateness for your situation.

Stop Smoking. Of all the chemical substances and pollutants that are harmful to your health, none is more deadly than tobacco. If you use any tobacco product, you are drastically shortening your life. And if you do not smoke but live with or work among smokers, they are drastically shortening your life and destroying your good health. There is no chemical abuse more harmful to your health, heart, and lungs than tobacco products and the smoke they produce. There are more than 4,000 poisons found in tobacco that all work together to seriously damage your body. It matters not whether you smoke a pipe, cigars, or cigarettes or chew or sniff tobacco, it still wreaks havoc on your health. Low tars, high tars, filtered—it doesn't matter. Tobacco is deadly poison to just about every tissue in your body and especially to your heart. Stop exposing yourself to tobacco products right now, not tomorrow or next week. Quit smoking now!

If you are not a smoker but live with a smoker or work with smokers who expose you to their side-stream smoke, then give them the Quit Smoking Now! program, found in the appendix of this book. Your exposure to their smoke is deadly and will prevent you from making a full turnaround in your health and lifestyle. If they refuse to quit smoking, then make them understand they must not smoke in your home or in your presence. If you work among smokers, make them understand that although they have every right to injure themselves, they must not pollute the same air that you have to breathe.

Perhaps you think these are strong demands, but you cannot afford to take the chance of breathing second-hand or side-stream smoke any more than you yourself can afford to smoke. What you must realize—and what you must make others realize—is that side-stream smoke, the smoke that comes off of the lit end of the cigarette, cigar, or pipe while it smolders, is far more toxic and deadly than the mainstream smoke that the smoker inhales and then blows out!

Stop abusing drugs and alcohol. Next to smoking, the most prevalent addiction in this country and the world is addiction to alcohol. When it comes to alcohol, we get mixed messages. There are those who will tell you, "A drink will benefit you by relaxing you and getting rid of your distress." One drink—not a very strong one—may relax you a little, may help dilate your blood vessels a little, and may help you to digest your next meal a little better. On the other hand, a strong drink, a second, third, or more drinks will have a depressant effect, constricting your blood vessels, retarding digestion, and causing severe gastric irritation. If you can limit yourself to a glass of wine or beer after work or before dinner, booze won't hurt you and indeed might do you good. However, if you're the type of person who can't stop with just one, two at the most, you might have a drinking problem. And if you do have a drinking problem, you have to stay away from alcohol completely.

Alcohol addiction affects about one in five people in the United States. It cuts across all social, economic, racial, professional, and educational backgrounds. It is equally distributed among the sexes. If drinking has caused you problems in the past, now is the time to get help. Your life depends on getting help.

If you do not have a problem with alcohol, even minimal consumption can be dangerous if you are on medication. The blood thinner Coumarin, for example, is much affected by alcohol consumption and may be thrown out of control by occasional partying. Be sure you discuss your drinking habits honestly with your physician if you are on any medication at all. And if you find you can't discuss your drinking honestly with others, you probably do have a drinking problem.

One area of drug abuse that is all too often overlooked is the misuse of prescription drugs. It is not uncommon anymore, especially among the over-fifty set, to become addicted to medications originally prescribed for justifiable reasons. It is essential that you review all your medications with your physician. This is especially true if you see more than one doctor for your overall health care. Too frequently, one medical advisor does not know what another is prescribing, and you could be taking medications that either counteract each other, potentiate one another, or cause one or the other to react differently than is intended. Always let each physician know what the other is doing. It is also wise to get all your prescriptions and medications at one pharmacy so that the pharmacist can monitor what you are taking and see the overall picture of your medical regimen. Your pharmacist can be your greatest ally when it comes to keeping you safe from prescription misuse and abuse.

Acetylsalicylic Acid (Plain Old Aspirin). Aspirin is among our oldest medications. It is without a doubt the most versatile and amazing medical discovery in history. Our parents, our grandparents, and most likely our great-grandparents took it for fever, pain, colds, flu, chills, strains, sprains, and for almost everything else if nothing specific was available. And in most cases it helped. We are just finding how remarkable this medication really is.

If I could give only one piece of medical advice to people, the following sentence would probably be the one I'd choose: anyone over the age of fifty who is not allergic to aspirin and who is not on a blood thinning medication should take one aspirin a day under his or her personal medical advisor's direction. I feel it will save and prolong more lives than any other advice or medical procedure in my arsenal of medical skills. That's a profound statement, but I believe it. Why? Well, one aspirin a day can increase your chances of surviving a heart attack by forty-seven percent. In addition, it dramatically reduces your chances of having that heart attack in the first place. It also dramatically reduces the chances of having a stroke, and it reduces the chances of a stroke leaving permanent damage. Should you, however, have a stroke and suffer serious damage, aspirin reduces the seriousness of the injury. Aspirin is linked to the prevention of several cancers and may slow or help prevent the onset of Alzheimer's disease. It also retards the onset of inflammatory diseases such as arthritis and joint diseases as well as the permanent damage they can do.

If aspirin tends to irritate your stomach, ask your medical advisor about enteric coated or buffered aspirin. Remember, if you are allergic to aspirin, if you have a bleeding problem, or if you take blood thinning or other incompatible medication, you are among the few who should not take one aspirin daily. Check with your personal medical advisor before starting any medication that you intend to take on a regular basis.

Anti-oxidants. Anti-oxidants are getting a lot of press these days. They are vitamins that reduce the cellular damage from certain carcinogens that circulate in our bodies. Among the anti-oxidants are beta-carotene, vitamins C and E, the hormone melatonin, and several others. Melatonin is a substance that occurs naturally in the body and is produced by the pineal gland. As we age, the secretion of melatonin is reduced, so some physicians advise supplementation in pill form. We have no way of measuring at what point, if ever, melatonin drops to a level that requires supplementation. As far as anyone knows, however, melatonin supplementation has no detrimental effect. The substance has not been extensively studied, but people who have taken it for many years have shown no ill effects. It is reported to have anti-aging properties in animals, but human studies have not yet declared it the fountain of youth. It does work in reducing jet lag, and for some sleep problems seems to work wonders. Low doses are adequate, probably one to three milligrams daily or less.

Beta-carotene, vitamins C and E, and most other antioxidants are found in fruits and vegetables. Proper nutrition should provide you with all you need. But most of us fail in proper nutrition, so as we age, supplementation isn't a bad idea. Beta-carotene is in the vitamin A group and is one of the few vitamins on which you can overdose. You should not take more than 25,000 units of beta-carotene per day. Vitamin E at 400 mg and C at 1000 mg should be sufficient supplementation for most.

Geriatric Dentistry. This is a new specialty in dentistry that most of us will have to investigate sooner or later. Does that mean you'll have to leave your old dentist? Not necessarily. He or she will probably take some special courses or study up on the new problems age brings to dentistry. The important thing is that you know there are some new problems on the horizon. Ask your dentist about them and what you can do to prevent them.

Among other things, we have a reduction in salivation as we age. Especially at night, our mucous membranes tend to dry leaving that horrible taste in our mouths. Saliva also helps keep our teeth and gums healthy, rinsing them and reducing bacteria. So as your saliva production decreases, you may become more susceptible to tooth decay.

Mandibular recession is another problem we face as

we age. The bones holding the teeth in place sometimes lose some of their mineral calcium. Calcium supplements may be effective in slowing this problem. The recession of the gums is another problem you might face, especially if you experience drying of the mucus membranes. As the gums recede, we are subject to root damage and decay.

There are a couple of preventive measures you can take to counteract these problems. First, floss, floss, floss. Good flossing will help eliminate impacted foods between the teeth and gums that nurture bacterial growth and plaque. Fluoride also becomes more important as we age to prevent damage to teeth and roots. Fluoride rinses are quite effective, as are fluoride toothpastes.

As our population ages, dental implants will become more and more common. This procedure is rapidly replacing dentures and bridge work. The procedure should become less costly and time consuming as it is perfected. In the meantime, take good care of your teeth so that implants can be avoided altogether. Discuss your dental future with your dentist. If you have any dental problems, get them taken care of now—before they lead to more difficult problems and have a chance to affect your general health.

Immunizations. As we grow older, we sometimes have more difficulty overcoming illnesses. Furthermore, serious and prolonged illnesses can start a downward spiral in our total well-being. We should take any steps we can to prevent such illnesses. Immunizations are one way of protecting our well-being and health.

Get a flu vaccie every fall. Contrary to what some people may say, a flu vaccine is very unlikely to make you sick. Every autumn and winter, flu kills thousands of people in the United States who could have been protected by a simple injection. Most of them are over sixty years old.

Getting into the habit of flu vaccinations will protect you now and prepare you for a healthy future.

Hepatitis A and B vaccines have recently become available. They are relatively expensive, but the diseases they protect you from are potentially lethal. If foreign travel is a part of your retirement, these immunizations are all the more important.

Meningococcal meningitis vaccine is available and protects against an infection that can cause permanent central nervous system damage, brain damage, and death. Streptococcal pneumonia vaccine gives lifelong protection from a potentially fatal lung disease. Tetanus/Diphtheria vaccine should be injected every ten years and anytime a deep puncture wound is acquired such as a bite or nail piercing. Typhoid is an especially important vaccination if you'll be traveling. It is now available in oral form, which is more effective than the shot.

Endemic diseases are diseases that are prevalent in certain areas of the world where you may be traveling. You should contact the Center for Disease Control (CDC) at (404) 332-4559 before any trip to inquire about regional endemic health problems and the immunizations and precautions you can take to protect yourself. These illnesses may include polio, yellow fever, malaria, cholera, and other exotic diseases. With proper protection and information, you should never have to fear travel and new experiences.

Just for the Ladies

There is no truth to the myth that Pap smears and pelvic examinations are no longer necessary after menopause. Ovarian, uterine, and cervical cancers kill too many women, and these are both detectable through timely examinations and treatable in most cases that are diagnosed early. Gynecologic examinations must be a yearly habit for every woman regardless of age. Forgetting is no excuse. Being too busy is no excuse. Let a birthday or anniversary remind you every year and do it a day before or after. Make a mammogram part of that same examination. Breast cancer can strike at any age, and early discovery gives you a high chance for cure. If you do not do breast self-exams once a month, ask your medical advisor to show you how and do it on the first day of each month.

Calcium supplementation is of particular importance to women, especially after menopause, to prevent osteoporosis and compression fractures. Supplementation should begin in the thirties or forties, but if you are past that age and haven't started, calcium supplementation should start today! If you drink lots of milk (skim) and or eat lots of cottage cheese (low fat), you may not need supplementation, but most women don't get sufficient calcium in their diets. Talk to your pharmacist or medical advisor to determine the best calcium supplement for you. Other medications available to fight and even reverse the bone loss of osteoporosis are estrogen therapy, calcitonin, sodium fluoride and alendronate (Fosomax). Discuss these therapies with your medical advisor.

Heart disease has been too long ignored in women. When we didn't live as long as we now do, women didn't develop heart disease as early as men, and it was thought they weren't as susceptible. That has changed, but the myth remains. In the postmenopausal years, women develop heart disease at a more rapid rate then men, and in their late sixties and seventies, they are very susceptible to heart attack and heart failure, especially now that they are smoking in such great numbers. Estrogen therapy is one method of prolonging the premenopausal protection. Quit smoking, exercise, and reduce your ingestion of saturated fats. Insist on the same cardiac attention from your medical advisor that he would give to a man your age. It must also be remembered that women do not always have the same classic heart attack symptoms as men. Women may experience pain in the back between the scapula; also, they may not experience the perspiration or the radiation of pain to the neck and left arm that are characteristic of heart attacks in men.

Just for the Men

Two problems men must watch out for are prostate problems and rectal cancer. Prostrate problems include infections and benign prostatic hypertrophy (BPH). BPH is a noncancerous enlargement of the prostate gland that almost all men have as they age. In an appreciable number of men, the growth of this gland causes some degree of obstruction to the normal flow of urine from the bladder. There are some medications now available to relieve this obstruction without having to resort to surgery. They are worth trying. If, however, they do not work, surgical intervention may be required to prevent complete obstruction. These procedures can include removal of the gland, boring out a portion of the gland along the urethra, using microwaves to shrink the gland, or placing a stint in the urethra to open it up (not unlike angioplasty).

Prostate cancer is a growing problem as men live longer. Fortunately it is a very slow growing cancer in most cases, and early detection offers a high percentage of cure. The key word is *early*. There are two main methods of screening for prostate cancer. One is the blood test PSA, the other is yearly rectal examination of the prostate. Both of these tests should be carried out yearly on every male over age forty-five. If either raises suspicions of prostate cancer, they should be followed up with an ultrasound examination and possibly a needle biopsy of the prostate.

Rectal and colon cancer are certainly not unique to men, but they are more prevalent in men than in women. Both should be checked yearly for signs of the disease, especially men. Again, the best chance for a cure is early detection. Early detection depends on a simple test for blood in your stools. It should be a yearly check.

For a long, healthy life, it is essential that you keep the good health you have now, take care of any problems that presently exist, and do all you can to discover any new problems in time to correct them. This requires a team effort between you, your dentist, your pharmacist, and your medical advisors. I emphasize *you* because you are the head of this team. They can't help you if you don't seek their help or follow their advice.

TEN

Your Life May Depend on Your Attitude

If there is one remarkable similarity among the primitive folks who live so long, it's the lack of distress and more important, anger, in their lives. I make a point to emphasize the word *distress*. Much has been written about stress and stress reduction in past years. But stress is not the problem. Distress and its resultant anger are what kill us Americans.

Stress is normal to life. It is what motivates us to get things done. It pushes us off dead center—makes us climb out of ruts. It's when we can't do anything about the stress that we run into problems. We become distressed and angry. And it is this distress and anger and their accompanying frustrations, irritations, feelings of futility, failure, and disappointment that destroy our health and shorten our lives.

For most of us distress and anger are the most difficult aspects of our lifestyles to eliminate or change. Too many of us have set goals that are too demanding, unrealistic, or even impossible for ourselves.

Fortunately, as we get older, most of us tend to mellow out a bit, and distress and anger become a little less of a factor in our lives. When crises such as life-threatening illness come along, they seem to help us put aside some of the crazy goals that have caused us so much distress in our lives. Such crises tend to help us reprioritize our lives and values. Hopefully, however, this chapter will help you reprioritize your life and values *before* the distress and anger that bring on life-threatening illness arise. You must learn to let distress and anger play a minimal role in your long, healthy, happy future.

What can we learn about avoiding distress and anger from our primitive friends? Let's take a look at what material things they have in comparison to us. To begin with, in each of the geographic areas we've discussed, the people have adequate food to nourish themselves. Nature has provided well for them. They eat properly and they have plenty. They don't have a problem clothing themselves. They don't dress fancy, but they keep warm and comfortable. They dress for the prevailing climate. In places where it gets cold they add a few layers and wrap up in blankets; where and when it's warm or hot, they strip down to the bare essentials. Patches generally don't bother them.

They have roofs over their heads. The roof may shelter a whole extended family of a dozen or more in two or three rooms, but they stay dry when it rains, warm when it snows, and shaded when the sun beats down. There's rarely a lock on the door because there's little to steal. They don't have much, but they don't crave much. What is important to them are the necessities—the food on their table, the clothes on their back, the roof over their heads, and the love and support of their extended family.

Now compare. Most of us have too much food on our tables. Our homes are much more than adequate. Our clothing is usually abundantly hung in closets, and we are able to communicate with loved ones even if they are many miles away. If we're so much better off, why are we so distressed and angry?

Perhaps it's those cravings. Now I'm certainly not suggesting that we give up all our material and modern conveniences. Far from it. I have nothing against the good life. But let's reexamine our desires and make sure what we crave is really as good as we think. Let's make sure the price we pay with distress isn't too high.

For example, in our society, most of us need a car. The pace of our lives and the distances we have to travel are too great for us to rely on walking to get from appointment to appointment. We can buy a car for around $9,000 that will usually get us where we want to go with reasonable reliability and comfort. We can buy a $90,000 car, and it will usually get us there with reasonable reliability and considerably more comfort—but probably not $81,000 worth of added comfort. But the prestige may be worth $81,000 to some of us. If we can afford it, the luxury car may be a source of joy and happiness. That's where the good life may indeed be good for you.

However, if putting out that extra eighty-one grand causes too much sacrifice, hardship, sleeplessness, and a heap of distress, that good life isn't good for you. It just can't be worth it. If it harms your health, rethink your priorities and values. Set a more realistic goal. Find another more affordable way to derive that prestige. I'd love to be able to drive a Rolls Royce Silver Shadow Convertible, but I know the worry would kill me. Instead, I bought a used 1970 Buick Skylark Convertible for under $2000. By the time I got it all restored I had less than $5000 tied up in it. It's a thrill to drive, lets me be a bit of a show off, makes me feel like I'm the envy of all those other folks in small, closed, new plastic cars. I get my prestige and kicks for about $140,000 less, even if it is a little shy of being a Silver Shadow.

Now is the best time for you to reprioritize your life. Take a realistic inventory of your values. Is being at the top of your profession as important to you now as it once might have been? Is being the richest guy in the hospital or cemetery really what you want out of life? Are you going to be able to enjoy all your material possessions, or would you be better off with a few less things and a lot more time to enjoy your life, family, and friends?

Stress vs. Distress

Stress, as I use it in this book, means a physical or mental tension, an uneasiness, irritation, or force that nudges you toward changing the status quo. It does not imply pain, grief, suffering, strain, or frustration. These characteristics I relegate to *distress*.

I use *stress* to signify that good restlessness that provokes you to action. Distress, on the other hand, is worry, frustration, agony, or pain that results when your actions don't work out as desired. That brings on anger, and anger is what will do you in. Anger is what will cause you hypertension, ulcers, heart attacks, strokes, and a host of other dread diseases.

If you were a world-class sprinter and had a shot at the Olympics, you would no doubt come under considerable stress prior to the tryouts. If that stress made you work out harder, resulting in top fitness and improving your chances, it would be good. If you felt no stress prior to the tryouts, you probably wouldn't push yourself to attain peak conditioning. On the day of the tryouts, you would probably feel the greatest stress, which would get your adrenalin flowing and add considerably to your success.

After the race you would be elated if you placed. All that stress of the previous weeks and months would have benefited you.

If, on the other hand, you lost, there would probably be considerable frustration and pain—distress and its accompanying anger. If you didn't have a mechanism to cope with your distress and anger, it could lead to depression, anxiety, feelings of failure, and eventually any number of physical and mental ailments.

Stresses remain beneficial as long as they provoke positive action. Once you let them turn to negative action or inaction or become worrisome and self-deprecating, you've got distress. If the loser of the Olympic trials turns his failure to make the team into positive action, he will be coping with his distress, turning it back into positive stress. He might decide to work harder and improve his performance in case one of the winners dropped out and he was elected to the team as an alternate. Perhaps he would decide the event wasn't for him and turn his energies to another event, such as the team relay. He might decide he was finished with competition, that it was fun while it lasted, but now it was time to turn to other goals. All these would be positive reactions to potential distress, defusing it by turning it into other motivating stresses.

When you have a setback, don't fret and stew about it. That does no good. Turn your energies in another direction, and return to your problem at a later time when you can face it objectively. Maybe work on a hobby or take a ride on your bike. Exercise is a great way to defuse distress, and you may be surprised at how often a solution to your distress will come to you spontaneously while your attention is diverted to more pleasant activities.

If your life is constantly filled with distress and anger, it is time to take a good look at your situation. This may require the help of an objective outsider, not necessarily a professional counselor, but a trusted friend, spouse, fellow employee, clergy, parent, or child. However, don't discount a professional if the need is there. Get whatever help you need to realign your goals, values, and dreams. Remember, nothing is worth the ruination of your health.

Reprioritizing and Realistic Goal-Setting

When we first start out in our adult life our priorities might be something like this:

1. Profession or job
2. Money
3. Acquiring property and material goods
4. Family
5. Avocations and recreation
6. Nationality, politics
7. Religion
8. Health

When we get older they may realign themselves more like this:

1. Family
2. Health
3. Religion
4. Avocation and recreation
5. Profession or job
6. Money
7. Acquiring property and material goods
8. Nationality, politics

That's quite a change. Sometimes we are so busy chasing after our goals that we don't even realize they've changed. We should take time out every few years or so and examine ourselves and adjust our goals to fit our new needs and dreams. If we don't make adjustments, we may find distress rising in every facet of our lives. Have you ever noticed how well adjusted most of those people are who change professions every few years? We tend to look at them as unstable, lost, irresponsible, and generally unsuccessful. But take another hard look at them. They probably spend a lot more time smiling than you do. Distress is not a big factor in their lives. They adjust to their needs by changing directions, trying new things, and making fresh beginnings. They cope well; they are survivors. They aren't anchored to rigid goals.

Spend a few days listing your real priorities in their proper order. Don't hesitate to move things around and experiment with several different orders. Nothing is etched in stone. But let me suggest you try placing health and recreation high on your list. Both are powerful distress and anger reducers.

Recreation

I've already mentioned recreation several times, but it deserves a place of its own in this program. Quality recreation time is a must for you. It should be providing the good times for which you live. Quality recreation is one of the best vehicles to strengthen your family relationships. It will help you solve your problems and thus reduce your distress and anger levels. Quality recreation is a powerful method of reducing hypertension.

What is quality recreation? It is different for each of us. It is the avocation you most enjoy. I want to emphasize the word *avocation*. Even if you happen to be one of those lucky people who work in a profession or job you truly love to do more than anything else in the world, you still need some form of recreation apart from your career. You have to be able to get away to something else. It's what prevents job burnout, and you can burn out on any job no matter how terrific it may be to you.

Find avocations you can really throw yourself into. Try to become dedicated to them. If golf is your thing, take the challenge and work at becoming the best golfer you can be. If painting or sculpture is for you, you don't have to become another Grandma Moses or Picasso, but work at becoming the best artist you can be. If you can't get hooked enough, seek out other avocations. You can't have too many, and eventually one will grab you. Remember, the best distress-reducing avocation is one that takes a lot of concentration, demanding that you get your mind off everything else. It has to be able to push your problems right out of your mind. It has to push its way right into the priority-one slot while you're engaged in its activities. Thus, an avocation that requires skill development and concentration on detail is all the better. Perhaps a good place to start is to think about some of the things you wanted to do when you were younger but thought you didn't have the time or finances to pursue. Recreational pursuits can be classified into mental, physical, and skilled. Ideally, a person could pick one from each group. If you can't think of a niche for yourself, the following suggestions may help.

Physical Avocations
Exercise. We've already learned that exercise is the best distress reducer. If you can find an avocation that requires vigorous body activity, all the better. This activity should

not take the place of your walking program, though. It must be in addition to your daily walking. Team sports, tennis, golf, hiking, bodybuilding, swimming, and gardening are all activities that fit into this category. Once your walking program has put you into adequate physical condition and your physician gives you the go ahead, these would all be good distress-reducing avocations.

Hiking. What could take your mind off distressing matters better than getting out in nature for a hike? Hiking is different from your daily walk in that it needn't be as vigorous or aerobic. The idea is to get out in an invigorating yet restful environment where your mind can wander along with your body.

Dancing. Ballroom dancing is making a real comeback these days with competitions and clubs popping up everywhere. Whether you would enjoy competing or just want to be able to cut a mean rug once in a while at parties or on nights out, dancing is a very healthy avocation, giving you a good workout while taking your mind off disturbing factors in your life. Dancing lessons are readily available almost anywhere.

Biking. If you have good bike paths available, give it a try. It can't take the place of your daily walking, but it makes an excellent additional activity. You should be able to rent a bike and give it a fair trial before investing in your own. Bicycles aren't cheap anymore, and the technology has probably changed considerably since the last time you rolled up your pants legs and took a turn.

Volunteer work. Nothing is as satisfying as doing volunteer work that helps others not as fortunate as yourself. This can be anything from shoveling an elderly neighbor's walk to going out into a remote village and building a needed clinic. There is no end to the type of work needed out there or organizations to help you get started.

Gardening. A friend of mine who lives in an apartment with no yard space is one of the most avid gardeners I've ever met. His apartment is a virtual greenhouse. Every window sill, shelf, and table has potted plants. He has more plants on his floor than most of us have in our gardens. I often wonder what he'd do if he had a yard. The point is that gardening can be a wonderful avocation, and anyone can get into it. You can get started with just a few pots and plants or even seeds. Gardening can be scaled to your own space and needs. There is no end to how far you can take this hobby. You can specialize in orchids, roses, cacti, succulents, wild flowers, herbs, vegetables, trees, fruits, or shrubs—or you can go for it all. You can even breed your own varieties. Get a little dirt under your nails and give it a fair try.

Camping. This is a fun and challenging way to travel and meet new and interesting people. You can back pack (after your walking program puts you into adequate physical condition) or drive to the thousands of campgrounds throughout the world. You can buy or rent a recreational vehicle and have the freedom of a modern day Gypsy or rough it with just a tent and sleeping bag. You might try taking a wilderness course to develop some real survival skills. Once you can break the bonds of hotels and motels, the world really becomes yours with limitless frontiers to explore.

Farming. If gardening isn't enough of a challenge for you, perhaps you'd like to be a weekend farmer. At first I thought this was a little far-fetched, but I was surprised to find that a lot of city folks have a few acres in the country that they own or rent for horses, cattle, turkeys, chickens, rabbits, sheep, goats, pigs, dogs, cats, and other critters. Some people grow fruits and vegetables. Some just fish their streams or ponds. If you don't want to raise anything, perhaps just having a weekend home on a few acres could take your mind off the distressing factors in your life.

Mental Avocations

Reading. No matter what other avocation you may choose, there are times when nothing beats a good book. Create time for yourself to get through some of those books you didn't have time for in the past. You might want to join a reading group and share your love for literature with new friends. And if good books are a passion, you may want to expand into collecting rare books. You might also consider doing volunteer work for your local library association.

Travel. A vacation is a great revitalizer. The main problem is that we can't usually take enough of them. As wonderful as it is to get away for two weeks or longer, frequent long weekends are probably better for us. When we come back from very long vacations, the distress caused by all the catching up we have to do may undo all the good our vacation did us. If you only get two weeks vacation (ten working days) you may do better by using them around holiday weekends and getting several four or five day trips a year. If you have a job that requires a lot of travel, consider taking a couple of days at the end of your business trip to save on travel costs and take your spouse along.

Learning. Today there are so many adult education courses offered by public schools, colleges, churches, synagogues, organizations, museums, galleries, and private institutions, you can study almost anything you want. Learning in itself is a wonderful hobby, but more importantly, it can introduce you to many other exciting activities and interests to pursue in the future. The old adage "you can't teach an old dog new tricks" isn't true. The problem is that too many of us old dogs just don't try. Put forth the effort and you can learn anything you want. And the more you learn, the easier it becomes.

Stamp collecting. This is a hobby you can apply yourself to in all degrees. Perhaps you want to limit yourself to stamps of one type, like sports stamps from all countries or stamps from all the places you've visited. Maybe you want to go in for investing in rare stamps. This avocation can be limited to your kitchen table or it can take you all over the world to stamp shows and conventions.

Collecting. Collecting anything, stamps, coins, art, antiques, old cars, rare books, whatever strikes your fancy, can be a wonderful avocation. Collecting can take you to all corners of the world, or it can bring the world to you. You'll meet other people with interests similar to yours, and you might stumble across some real treasures. Most important, the study, travel and challenge of collecting will go a long way to reducing the distress of your daily life.

Skill Avocations

Bowling. You might think bowling should fall under exercise, but as an exercise it doesn't build up much of a sweat. However, as a game of skill and a way to get out with people and take your mind off distressing problems, it has plenty going for it. Bowling promotes a spirit of competition, and honing all the fine points will require complete concentration. You can join a league to add excitement and good fellowship or you can just challenge yourself with constant improvement. One thing you have to watch out for in most bowling alleys, however, is side-stream smoke. More and more bowling alleys are now seeing the benefit of starting smoke-free leagues and making some of their lanes non-smoking. If you can't find one of these more progressive places, suggest the idea to the manager at a local alley.

Music. I'm not suggesting you be only a spectator. You're never too old to take music lessons. Did you ever wish you'd taken up an instrument as a kid? Perhaps you did take lessons but didn't pursue it as far as you would have liked. There's no better time than the present to remedy that mistake. I know a fifty-eight-year-old executive who took up the French Horn two years ago and has become quite proficient at it. He has also become involved with Barber Shop singing and travels to national and international competitions. Music has become a top priority in his life, and he'll tell you he's never enjoyed life more.

Carpentry. If you are talented with your hands and have a creative tendency, consider carpentry or model building. It can be very satisfying and distress reducing to see your own creations come to life. This is an avocation in which you will constantly improve and develop new skills. And if woods don't turn you on, perhaps metals will. I know an executive from a large wrecking company who started welding together bits and pieces of junk one day and today is a sculptor of note. His avocation opens whole new vistas to him as he travels to showings of his works.

Painting. Water colors, oils, acrylics, chalk, crayons, pencils, ink, and charcoal, all await you to give them a try. You may never sell a picture, but that isn't the main purpose. There are few activities that can be more absorbing than to dabble with paints. You don't have to possess great talent to enjoy art. A few lessons and you'll be able to express yourself surprisingly well on paper or canvas. Art skills can be learned to a point where they become at least self-satisfying and totally absorbing—and that's the main idea. But don't be surprised if you discover a hidden talent once you begin to nurture your creativity.

Sculpture. Who didn't enjoy modeling clay as a child? Why not try the adult version? Sculpture, ceramics, origami, welding, carving, and papier-mâché are just a few of the ways for you to create in three dimensions.

Writing. There is no more forgiving art form than writing; anyone can do it! And just about everyone has said at one time or another, "I'd like to write a book about. . ." Well, now's the time to get started. Writing will completely absorb your mind. You can't do it and worry about anything else that could be causing you distress. If nothing else, write your family history to hand down to your kids and grandchildren. But if you have the least desire to write something else—a book, articles, poetry, lyrics, scripts— have at it! The more you write, the more you'll improve, and the more pleasure you'll get from it.

Investing. Investing may at first seem like a distressing activity, but that's only if you invest more than you can afford to lose. Some people know what they are doing and often come up winners. The fact is, if investing isn't what you do for a living and you can afford to take the plunge, it can be an excellent avocation. If you are the type who enjoys researching companies, knows the ins and outs of the markets, and can afford the gamble, then investing can be a legitimate hobby for you. This is especially true if your investments include coins, stamps, art, or antiques.

Entrepreneurship. If you qualify for the investing hobby category, then this is just a step beyond. Just don't get into something that adds to your distress.

Teaching. In all the years you've lived and experienced, you've learned a lot more than you realize. You have skills and knowledge that others can learn from.

Teaching is one of the most satisfying and enjoyable experiences you can imagine. Check around your local schools and universities. Many have adult continuing education programs that offer any number of courses, such as ballroom dancing, word processing, bookkeeping, entrepreneurship, languages, and writing. You can't have had such an uninteresting life that you don't have something to pass on to others. Look upon it as an obligation to share your expertise with others.

Golf. Golf, like bowling, deserves special mention. It has little value as an aerobic exercise, but it is a skill activity that is constantly challenging and that makes an excellent hobby. It takes you out of doors, expands your friendships, absorbs your attention, and helps you to stay limber. If you can walk the course, all the better. And you're never too old to take it up. My mother-in-law still played weekly when she was in her eighties—after she had open heart surgery.

Fishing. Fishing is an international pastime. You can practice this art anywhere in the world. From trolling to fly casting to deep sea fishing and spear fishing, it's always a challenge. You can get a workout fishing or you can snooze on the bank of a stream or lake waiting for a strike, but whichever you do, it is a good distress-reducing activity. Fishing is a great family avocation, but you can also sneak off by yourself if solitude is what you need.

Flying. This is a rich man's or woman's hobby, but if you can afford it, flying is an adventure in itself. You may choose powered aircraft, or you can go in for gliding if you live where there are good air currents and thermals. If you're really adventurous, you might even go in for ballooning or hang gliding. This is certainly not for everyone, but if it's something you've always wanted to do, why not now?

Boating. Boating is among the world's most practiced pastimes. You can spend millions on a yacht or just a few hundred bucks on a canoe. I'll never forget the sign I saw on a yacht docked in the Bahamas: "The greatest two days in a boat owner's life are the day he buys his boat and the day he sells it!" What the sign didn't say was that most boat owners sell their boats only to buy bigger ones!

Photography. Photography is an activity that works in combination with almost any other hobby you might choose. With today's amazing and inexpensive automatic cameras, almost anyone can be an expert photographer. And with the easy-to-use video cameras, you can even be your own movie producer.

The above listing is just a scratch on the surface of all the leisure time activities you can get involved in. Of course, there is a great deal of overlap in their categorization. Many activities require skill and have a mental and physical focus as well. The most important thing is that you get involved. Don't limit yourself to just one avocation. The more you engage in, the broader your interests will be and the better, more relaxed you'll be for it. Above all, learn to enjoy life. Reprioritize! The things that you've let distress you all of your life probably were never as important as you made them. We create most of our distress, and we can rid ourselves of it with just a little effort.

ELEVEN

Sex after Fifty

Now that you've made a commitment to good health and you have years of healthy, active years ahead of you, you can start concentrating on how you want to spend those years, what sorts of things you want to focus your energies on. In addition to developing new interests and avocations as you realign your priorities for a long, healthy life, there are certain things you'll likely want to *continue* developing and enjoying. One thing you probably will want to keep enjoying is intimacy with your spouse or partner. Although some of you might think people lose interest in sex as they age, it's just not true. Many people, in fact, think sex gets better and better as time goes on. Let's take a look at what's myth and what's fact.

Myth: After a certain age, people just aren't interested in sex.

Fact: The great majority of people are sexually in-clined until they die, regardless of age. Sadly, opportunity often decreases with the declining health or death of mari-tal partners. But among couples who enjoy longevity together, the joys of sex usually continue. Frequency may diminish a bit, but this will vary from a few times a month to a few times a week. Regardless of the frequency, most couples will tell you that the quality and satisfaction of their sexual relations increases with time. Most important, they will tell you that their love has deepened and that their sex is more expressive of that love than before now. Maturity brings a great deal to sexuality, because we constantly get to know our partners better. In the process, we gain insight into one another's needs, likes, and desires. Also, as we mature we tend to take more time with sex both in foreplay and in the act itself. The frequency may diminish a little, but intimate time together increases. Also other aspsects of foreplay tend to become more important and enjoyable—cuddling, intimate looks, jokes, memories of shared experiences. Activities such as petting, touch, and massage may also become more meaningful parts of our intimate expression. Women sometimes become orgasmic for the first time after menopause.

Myth: After all these years there just isn't anything new to look forward to.

Fact: You may think you've tried it all, but odds are you haven't. Actually, for most couples, the "same old routine" has become routine because it is what satisfies. But when couples talk freely, it is surprising what fantasies can be played out and what experimentation can be tried. Ask at your local video store about how many more mature people are renting explicit movies. They are stimulating to lots of couples, and to those who have been more conservative, they can be quite educational. Surprised? Well, just as many mature couples are buying the latest electronic devices and massagers of all shapes and forms for mutual stimulation and foreplay. Yes, there are lots of discoveries out there for those of you who really think you've tried it all. The best way to get some excitement and spice into your life is to talk with your partner about each other's needs, curiosities, fantasies, and desires.

Myth: The spirit is willing but the flesh is too weak.

Fact: Although as we age the potential for chronic illness increases, few chronic illnesses interfere with sexual function. The most common dysfunctional problem men of all ages suffer is the inability to maintain an erection, and few chronic illnesses cause this problem. In other words, even men in their sixties and seventies who have chronic illnesses are generally able to maintain erection adequately enough to enjoy fulfilling sexual relationships. Probably ninety percent of impotency problems can be easily treated nonsurgically. If you have such a problem, don't get the idea that it's "normal at my age." Impotence is never normal at any age. See your physician or a urologist and find out the reason for your problem. If your physician says not to worry, "it's normal at your age," get another opinion. Keep looking until you find a doctor who can give you a real reason for your dysfunction, and then get that problem treated!

Some women lose their ability to lubricate adequately as their estrogen levels drop, but there are numerous lubricating products that help, and for women who use estrogen replacement therapy, this problem rarely arises. Interestingly, women who remain sexually active—even without hormone therapy—seem to experience this problem less often.

Occasionally, in both men and women, adverse reactions to medications can diminish sexual function. Simply changing medications can often resolve these problems. Sadly, too many physicians are not sensitive to the importance of sex in the lives of people over fifty and don't take these side effects into consideration when prescribing.

The better your general health, the more interest you will have in a good sex life. Good nutrition, exercise, getting ailments taken care of when they appear, avoiding excess alcohol and tobacco (both of which diminish sexual drive), and avoiding certain medications can all add to your sexual prowess well into the second half of life.

Myth: There is no need to treat sexual dysfunction in people past a certain age.

Fact: Certainly when sexual dysfunction is caused by medication, every effort should be made to change that medication to one more agreeable to the patient's or couple's sexuality needs. Again, you can't depend on your physician's sensitivity in a case like this. If you've noticed a drop in your or your partner's libido or fulfillment and one or both of you are on medication, discuss the problem with your physician or pharmacist. There are, of course, numerous physical reasons for changes in libido and sexual performance. Most are not due to age per se but are caused by age-related illnesses. And though some of these conditions can't be treated, it's a mistake to believe that, despite our desires, it's all over because of age.

That is often the furthest thing from the truth. Even in the case of chronic diseases that have no cure, just getting them under control can often put fire back in the furnace when there's snow on the roof! In fact, changes in libido are often a very good and early indication that a chronic health problem has gotten out of control and needs the attention of your physician. If there has been a sudden and drastic change in your lust and love life, do not take it for granted that it is a normal part of aging. It probably isn't! Age may slowly bring about a change in quantity, but not in quality. Sudden and abrupt changes are usually a sign of some other problem that may well be correctable.

Myth: Most chronic illnesses make a satisfactory sex life impossible.

Fact: In some cases of serious or chronic disease, patients can become hypersexual. Alzheimer's patients often lose some of their old inhibitions or revert to a time when they were very sexually active and respond with renewed fervor. Survivors of cancer or other life-threatening experiences will often tell you that since their illness they have had a renewed interest and ardor where sex is concerned.

When certain physical health problems *do* cause impotence or irreversible sexual dysfunction, couples often find satisfaction in other sexual or nonsexual endeavors, such as sharing a love for music, nature, or books, talking, remembering, holding hands, touching, dancing, walking, caressing, stroking, cuddling, and petting.

Myth: Homosexual relationships are mostly platonic after fifty.

Fact. Everything that has been said above regarding sex after fifty is the same for those who are gay. In fact, many gay men and women seem to come out of the closet in later life. Perhaps it is because their kids have grown up or they've become widowed or divorced and have an opportunity to turn to a lifestyle they've denied. Or perhaps lifecycle changes have helped them find their true sexual identity. Whatever the cause, this lifestyle change in later years may open up a whole new sexual experience for them.

Sexual dysfunction and impotence in later years are the exception, not the rule. If you've had a reasonably normal sexual life until now, you should look forward to continued improvement as you grow older. Quantity may diminish a bit, but quality should grow constantly. What is normal quantity? Whatever keeps you and your partner satisfied. There are couples in their eighties and older who are satisfied with conjugal events a few times a year, while other octogenarians—and older—still enjoy one or more romps a week. Both are normal! And as for quality, if it leaves you looking forward to next time, everything must be fine.

TWELVE

It's All in Your Head: Staying Mentally Sharp

When we get into our forties and fifties we sometimes feel our memories are beginning to slip. We remember a fantastic meal we had at an event fifteen years ago as if it were just yesterday, but we can't remember whether we ate lunch today, much less what we had. We're always misplacing things or seeing someone we recognize but can't name. Or you'll start to tell someone about a great movie you saw last week only to realize you can't remember the title—you might even have a hard time remembering what it was about. At first it's a bit annoying, something to joke about. But perhaps that joking is to cover up some fears. "Am I getting Alzheimer's?" you may wonder. "Is this the beginning of senility? . . . Is it all down hill from here? . . . Will I be able to keep my job if my mind goes?"

Dispelling Myths

There are indeed many myths out there regarding the aging mind. But age has little to do with mental capacity and ability. True, there are a number of diseases that cause serious and unpreventable deterioration of the mind, such as Alzheimer's, senility, organic brain syndrome, certain circulatory problems, and a few other neuro-degenerating ailments, but most of these problems are not purely age dependent. The fact is that the aging mind is, for the great majority of us, very capable of memory, learning, and sharpness.

The mind is like an amazing computer with trillions of neurological circuits. In fact there is a huge reserve of billions of neurons with a trillion connections in each cubic centimeter. The brain is far superior to any computer man has ever put together. It is slower in some processes, but for the most part it can do things no manmade computer will probably ever be able to accomplish. Even when there is a biological ailment, the mind in most cases can do amazing things to restore itself or compensate for lost functions. But for most of us our little memory glitches are not memory *losses* but just a misplacement of information we probably didn't think important enough to catagorize properly—like misfiling in a computer or cabinet. The information is there, you just have to find how you filed it. In most cases it is a matter of carelessness in filing rather than an inability to learn or remember.

Let's take a closer look at some of the myths about the mind after fifty:

1. *Myth:* "You can't teach an old dog new tricks!" The older we get the harder it is to learn. *Not true!* We can and do learn to the day we check out. Each new experience teaches us something. In fact many things are easier learned now than when we were younger because we have a wealth of experience to found our new information on. I'm now sixty-three, and as a physician frequently covering emergency rooms, urgent care centers, and the occasional disaster situation, I must constantly take continuing medical education courses to keep myself abreast of new techniques and to keep my credentials and medical licenses in force. Every course I take has physicians of all ages participating, and we "mature" docs do every bit as well as the "youngsters." In fact, we frequently learn the new material faster and easier because of our experience in the field and our constant dialogue with peers.

Look around on college campuses today and you'll see many a senior citizen taking classes on every subject under the sun, and if you ask their younger classmates, they'll tell you the older students give them stiff competition and tend to raise the class average. Many "retired" folks give up their jobs just to start new careers, having to gain new skills and knowledge—which they usually do with little difficulty. Aging is not a downhill ride. Older people have talents, skills, abilities, knowledge, and experience that outshine the younger set easily. We have greater vocabularies, have greater understanding of written and spoken concepts, have a greater capacity for reasoning and good judgment, all because of a wealth of experience that we simply don't have in youth. There is a reason why masters classes are taught by older artists to younger musicians, why the top ranks in the military are older, why corporate leaders have grayer heads than middle management. Experience comes with age, as does wisdom. You won't lose that as long as you continue to use it.

2. *Myth:* Our brain cells disappear by tens of thousands a day so that when we are older we have few left. *Not true!* Yes, we lose cells all through the body and replace them with new ones, a process that begins at birth and continues through life. The brain also loses and gains cells continually. But cells do not cause thought, learning, memory, reflex, or function. Connections and circuits do.

These circuits do not break just because new cells, which are their building blocks, are constantly replacing old, used up ones. We are always building new connections as we learn and reinforcing old pathways when we think and practice our skills. If one of these pathways is interrupted, the brain is perfectly capable of bypassing the "defective" pathway with a new or alternate route. That's why exercising the mind is as important as exercising the muscles of the body. Challenge keeps it functioning efficiently.

3. *Myth:* Forgetfulness is the first sign that something is wrong with your brain, and the mind just goes down hill from there. *Not true!* Actually, there is very little that we forget completely, but if we don't use certain information for a while we tend to "put it out of our mind." It gets filed away to make room for the things more important and current to us. What we "forget" or remember has more to do with priorities than with the ability to retain. It is important that we are able to keep at hand only what is important and put what is no longer vital on the "back burner."

4. *Myth:* If you think you have a biological reason for your memory losses, you probably have Alzheimer's or some other disabling disease. *Not true!* People who have a biological cause for their memory problems are rarely aware of it. Biological memory problems do their damage before you yourself notice. By the time a disease like Alzheimer's affects your memory, you are beyond noticing or caring. It is relatives and friends who notice the problems. And if it is early Alzheimer's, there is considerable hope. Alzheimer's research is advancing at such a pace now that it is likely that by the year 2000 we will see drugs to dramatically slow the progress of this disease.

5. *Myth:* Once your memory starts to go, it can only get worse. *Not true!* Remember, priority has more to do with memory than does mental ability or capacity. We go through many changes and periods in our lives. Our interests and priorities change. We may feel forgetful and mentally inactive for periods when we are bored, undergoing value changes, or going through life-cycle changes. When we start in a new direction and different things begin to interest us, we become mentally alert and sharp again. Moods, too, have a lot to do with our mental abilities, and we must be motivated to be mentally alert, active, and retentive.

Apathy to Atrophy... Stimulation to Sharpness!

As in the muscles of the body, disuse will cause atrophy in the mind. But brain stimulation, as with muscle stimulation, can stop the atrophy and reverse the process to growth and increased mental function. We must keep ourselves interested in what goes on around us. The more we get out and mingle with the world the more stimulation we get. Stimulation—experiences—lead to excitement, interest, curiosity, and renewed learning. Mental activity of any kind will improve memory and mental skills. If all we do is sit and watch TV, there won't be much worth remembering.

Your Memory Is Better Than You Think

Really? So why can't I remember simple things like names, where I put things, things the kids tell me I did on trips, and . . . I can't remember what else? It's those priorities again. As we get older we know more people. We can't remember them all, there are too many other important things to store and file for quick access. Those less important names we file away in hard-to-reach corners. If you really forgot them there would be no recognition when someone gave you the name ("Oh, yeah, now I remember!"). "Oh yeah!" means you didn't really forget! And as we get older we possess more things, which means we have more things to misplace. But the main reason we forget where we put down the keys is because we were doing something else that occupied our minds at the time we laid them down. Everyone does it at all ages. We are just more sensitive to our misplacements.

And when your kids have a laugh about something you did when we took them to Disneyland, and you can't remember it, how is that explained? Priorities again! That trip surely meant a lot more to them that it did to you, no matter how big a thrill it might have been. And chances are you had more things on you mind at the time than the kids did.

Exercising the Mind

Get out of your retirement mode. Even before we're retired, we often tend to slow down physically and mentally. Don't let it happen to you. Instead of thinking about slowing down, realign your priorities for your next *lifestyle change*—you're not retiring but embarking on new ventures to broaden your horizons and interests, pursuits and experiences. Think about adult education, travel, reading, writing, music, hobbies, nature, and all the things you wanted to do but never had the time for. Consider getting another degree—maybe a new career. You have time. Lots of time. A half a lifetime—the whole second half.

Also, there are strategies to help keep your memory sharp. Pay attention when you are trying to remember something. Don't let distractions get in the way. Focus on what you are trying to recall or what you are trying to put into memory. Distraction is probably the biggest reason for forgetfulness. Focus! Take notes. Make lists. You did that when you were younger; continue to make lists now. Another reason older people have difficulty with names is that they are often less interested in meeting new people. Take an interest in the people you meet. Repeat names when introduced and use them in conversations.

Keeping Up the Circulation and Aeration

To keep the mind functioning at peak performance you have to keep up your physical fitness as well. The brain uses more oxygen than any organ in the body. To keep it well nourished you have to keep oxygenated blood flowing at full force. That means keeping up a healthy cardiopulmonary system. A healthy heart is necessary to pump the blood, and healthy lungs have to load that blood with fresh, clean oxygen. A good aerobic exercise program, such as the one described in this book, is essential.

Don't Poison Those Delicate Fibers

There are many poisons waiting to destroy those delicate fibers and synapses that produce mental function, including alcohol, tobacco, over-the-counter drugs, prescription drugs, hard drugs, and pollution. For example, tobacco has hundreds of lethal chemicals in its smoke that attack nerve and brain cells as they do all the cells of the body. Because the health and function of the brain is vitally dependent on a huge supply of clean, fresh oxygen, the displacement of this vital oxygen by smoke has an immediate detrimental effect on your brain.

Excessive alcohol use leads directly to organic brain syndrome, a severe form of dementia. Alcohol should be used only in moderation. Marijuana and hard drugs have a direct biological effect on brain cells that can be described only as devastating. Prescription and over-the-counter medications vary greatly in their effect on mental function and memory. None should be used without the knowledge, supervision, and direction of your physician or pharmacist. Your pharmacist is perhaps your greatest ally in your efforts to reach your maximum life potential. You may go to several physicians for various aspects of your health, but you should use only one pharmacist. He can monitor all the medications you are taking in case several doctors prescribe medications that can potentiate or work against one another. Also, you should always tell your doctors what medications you are taking, whether they are over the counter or prescribed by other physicians.

Use It, You Won't Lose It!

Remember, exercising your mind helps keep it sharp. How does one exercise the mind? Get creative! There are many organizations out there to help you exercise the mind in inventive ways. Explore community programs, church programs, art programs, writing clubs, travel clubs, and organizations such as Elderhostle, AARP, YMCA, American Heart Association, American Stroke Association, Alzheimer's Association, Parkinson's Disease Association, Diabetes Association, etc. There are two ways to use these and other organizations, both of which are beneficial to you. One is to utilize their services, and the other is to volunteer for them.

As we grow older, our minds accumulate a wealth of experience and knowledge. It is our choice to find ways to use it for the good of ourselves and others or to let it dissipate and go to waste.

THIRTEEN

The Economics of Age

When Social Security was introduced more than half a century ago, no one expected you and 75,000 others to live a full century. You were supposed to start getting paid your pension at sixty-five and die at around sixty-eight. Well, I'm not about to cooperate with that idea of longevity, and I doubt you're interested in it either! The consequences of our long lives, however, show up in our finances.

If you fall anywhere near the average, you'll get somewhere around $500 to $600 a month, around $1,000 to $1200 per couple, if you retire at sixty-two years of age. To supplement that, you'll be able to earn around $8,000 to $9,000 a year, after which you'll have to pay back one dollar for every two you earn over your limit. Retire at sixty-five, and they'll pay you back at a rate of $600 to $700 per month, and you'll be able to earn a little more before they start taking it back. At age seventy, you'll be able to earn all you want without payback—if they don't change the rules by then. In any case, life on Social Security ain't gonna be easy!

So what can you do about it?

Hopefully you have some savings, a Keogh Plan, a 401K, a pension from work, stocks, bonds, a home with a paid mortgage—some kind of nest egg squirreled away. Let's look at the options you have for retirement income whether your answer is yes or no.

Actuarial tables of insurance companies say that a man retiring at age sixty-five can look forward to at least fifteen years of retirement, and women who retire at the same age can expect more than twenty years. These are conservative estimates. With the lifestyle changes people are making today, with the advances in medical care and growth in other technologies, the sixty-five-year-old who exercises, follows sensible nutrition, and doesn't smoke and poison his or her system with other chemical abuses should far exceed those predictions. Don't forget, those actuarial tables are made up of averages of those who make wise lifestyle choices and those who make bad choices. In contrast with those who make the bad choices and die under the ages of seventy or eighty, there are those who balance the average and far outlive those actuarial-table ages. Assuming that those of you reading this book are making the wise choices, it would be wise to plan for a retirement life span of fifty years or more!

So how much money will you need to carry you through life in the style to which you're accustomed? A rule of the thumb that pops up in most books on retirement states that on the average, the cost of living during retirement is about seventy to eighty percent of what you need before retirement. Why so much less? Most retirees no longer have to put kids through school, they have their home paid off, they carry less insurance, they need less new clothing, they can get by on one car, they entertain less, they make fewer major purchases, they don't have as many loans with high interest rates, etc. Again these are averages—some will do better while others will exceed these expenditures.

You should explore a number of avenues when preparing for your future financial needs.

Take Inventory

What are your assets? Ask the Social Security Administration for an estimate of your social security payments if you and your spouse retired at ages sixty-two, sixty-five, and seventy. It could vary between $500 to $1200 a month for each of you, depending on how long you worked and how much you contributed during those years.

Estimate what you will get from pensions from employers (IRAs, 401Ks, savings, investments, royalties, etc.). Add to these estimates the value of your home equity. The sum of all these figures will be roughly what you will have to rely on in retirement. How long will it carry you? How can you stretch it? What can you do to supplement it? These are the next questions you have to ask yourself. Don't panic quite yet. It may not be as bad as it seems.

Study

Your local library probably has dozens of books on financing your retirement. Check them all out and study them. Although a lot of them will tell you how to retire well if you're a millionaire, some will address the problems facing those of us who didn't make it to even a quarter of that wealth. They will show you how to figure your true net worth, and it may surprise you to learn that you are better off than you think. Furthermore, if you are now around fifty, they will suggest how to prepare yourself in the next twelve to twenty years to get the maximum nest egg for retirement.

Get Good Advice

There are lots of financial advisors out there waiting and willing to give you advice on how to maximize your future fortune. Some are good at what they do, but many are totally unqualified. Get referrals from people who have had good success with their financial advisors. Shy away from an advisor who benefits from commissions by buying and selling your stocks and bonds. Ask your accountant for advice and referrals. Listen to the advice, then weigh it and think about it before you jump. Discuss it with others whose opinions you respect. Most advice is cheap, but good advice is worth its weight in gold.

Consider Later or Partial Retirement

If you like the work you're doing and are healthy, seriously consider delaying your retirement. You have lots of years between now and the end of your century for golf, fishing, and travel. Every extra year you work you can enlarge that nest egg rather than draw on it. And remember, if you take retirement at seventy instead of sixty-two or sixty-five, your social security payment grows—if they don't change the rules. You have to consider that possibility.

If you don't like the job you have or don't want to put in all the hours you now do, consider partial retirement. Look at a new job with less pressure and hours. Perhaps there is something you've always wanted to try, but you could never afford to take the pay cut. Now may be the chance you've waited for. You could be doing something new you've always wanted to do, yet still building or at least supplementing your nest egg. It's worth considering and discussing with your financial advisor.

Retrain and Retrench

If you take social security and don't want to earn over your allotted limit of income, you may want to consider retraining or developing new skills for the time when you will again be allowed to earn more. Perhaps you would be interested in real estate school, training for a stock broker's license, or some other job that lets you pick and choose your hours and your earning potential. Think about teaching. Take a hard look at volunteer work. Also, volunteer work can often lead to part-time paid work either through the organization you are volunteering for or through connections you make.

Retirement Does Not Mean Poverty

In the past, retirement has too often raised the image of an old fogey rocking in a chair watching the world go by watching TV soaps and sitcoms. That's not what your next thirty to fifty years should be all about. Retirement should be a whole new opportunity, not a dead end. It's as much a time to start a new career, pursue hobbies that can turn into careers, travel, and in general become more active than you've ever been before. The worst thing you can do is just sit there and watch your savings dwindle.

You've spent probably half a century getting to where you are today. In that time, you've learned a lot. Now use that hard earned knowledge to make the second half an active, productive, happy time of life!

APPENDICES

Charting Your Progress

Month	1	2	3	4	5	6	7	8	9
Resting Pulse									
Blood Pressure									
Waist Size									
Thigh Size									
Hip Size									
Chest Size									
Neck Size									
Body Fat %									

Measure these parameters once a month and record them to follow your improvement.

Your Walking Record:
When you first begin walking, walk as far and as long as is comfortable for up to one hour if you can. Record the time and distance at the end of each week. Then try to add to the time and the distance each day until you are able to walk briskly for an hour with confidence.

WEEK #	1	2	3	4	5	6	7	8
Time Walked								
Distance Walked								

You will probably be able to walk briskly for one hour long before eight weeks have passed. As soon as you are able to walk briskly for an hour, begin taking your pulse at the middle of your walk and once more just before you begin your cool down. Take your pulse for ten seconds and multiply it by six. Average the two results and record it once a week. On the day you take your recording pulses, also record your time and distance for that day. Gradually increase your walking speed until you are able to maintain your Ideal Exercise Pulse Rate for your age for one hour.

WEEK #	1	2	3	4	5	6	7	8	9	10
Distance in One Hour										
Walk Pulse Rate										

As your physical condition improves, you will notice that the distance you walk in one hour to maintain the same Ideal Exercise Pulse Rate will lengthen. After you achieve a high level of physical fitness, your improvement will slow and you may want to record your progress only once a month.

MONTH #	1	2	3	4	5	6	7	8	9	10
Distance in One Hour										
Walk Pulse Rate										

MONTH #	11	12	13	14	15	16	17	18	19	20
Distance in One Hour										
Walk Pulse Rate										

Quit Smoking Now! Program

QUIT SMOKING NOW!™ is a program to help you break your smoking addiction. As with any other addiction, it is important for you to admit you have an addiction to tobacco products. Denial is the biggest obstacle to breaking your addiction to tobacco use.

Why Cold Turkey?

Because tobacco use is an addiction, the best way to "kick" your habit is to quit "cold turkey." That may sound difficult and cruel and may intimidate you, but kicking cold turkey is indeed the best way to quit smoking. In fact, more than ninety percent of those who successfully become nonsmokers do it cold turkey.

Why is cold turkey the best way to stop smoking? Smoking is an addiction to the chemical nicotine, and as with any addiction, tapering off only keeps the addiction alive. No one who has had experience in alcohol addiction treatment would ever suggest tapering off booze. Each drink only increases the desire or need to continue drinking. The same is true of smoking. Each smoke makes your body crave another smoke. Tapering off only prolongs the agony and strengthens the addiction.

The "Kick Cold Turkey" Ceremony

It is important that you make a firm commitment to quit your smoking habit. You have to make an investment in quitting. One way to do this is to get rid of all your smoking paraphernalia. After all, if you are committed to quitting, you certainly don't need to keep anything related to smoking. If you're not willing to get rid of your smoking paraphernalia, you obviously aren't too serious about becoming a nonsmoker for the rest of your life. That is, after all what it means to quit smoking—becoming a nonsmoker for the rest of your life. Nonsmokers do not need smoking paraphernalia. Nonsmokers do not need ashtrays, humidors, pipes, pipe cleaners, tobacco, cigars, cigarettes, lighters, tobacco pouches, snuff, chewing tobacco, cuspidors, etc. The "kick cold turkey" ceremony is where you get rid of all these trappings. It means that if you ever go back to smoking you'll have to make an active decision to reinvest in smoking supplies, and that in itself may be just enough of a deterrent to keep you from "falling off the wagon!"

Gather everything that is part of your smoking habit and throw it into the trash. If you hold back, you are only hurting yourself. The more you get rid of, the greater your commitment, and the better your chances for success. When I quit, I gave away a brand new box of cigars with only one of them smoked. That was about a $35 commitment. In addition, I got rid of a humidor and about seven pipes, an additional $180 commitment. I also cleaned my home and office of all ashtrays, lighters, and smoking gadgetry, which brought my total commitment to roughly

$280. By the time my wife had the drapes and furniture cleaned of the smoke residue and smell, my investment in quitting was well over $350. Believe me when I tell you, that made it difficult to consider a return to smoking. Your success in quitting makes the sacrifice of all that paraphernalia well worthwhile.

Now that you have discarded your smoking paraphernalia, you are a nonsmoker! Congratulations! You are a nonsmoker! It is important that you think of yourself as a nonsmoker! Realize it—you are a nonsmoker!

Smoking or Any Other Tobacco Use Is An Addiction!

Let's reemphasize, "Smoking or tobacco use is an addiction!" Smoking is an addiction to the chemical substance nicotine. Nicotine addiction is considered by many authorities to be as strong as an addiction to heroin or opium. That means that now is the best time to quit, because tomorrow your addiction will be stronger. But don't let the addiction facts intimidate you. The half-life of nicotine in your system is relatively short, and addiction withdrawal to nicotine is usually over within forty-eight hours. Physical withdrawal, however, is not the only difficulty you will experience in quitting. There are two other factors involved with smoking that you must understand: *psychological dependence* and *habituation*. Let's take a more detailed look at the differences between addiction, psychological dependence, and habituation.

Addiction
Addiction involves an actual biological physical craving by the cells of your body for the chemical substance nicotine. Nicotine is found only in tobacco as a non-additive.

The longer and more frequently you use tobacco products in any form, the stronger your addiction becomes. The stronger your addiction becomes, the more intense your withdrawal symptoms are likely to be. Once you are addicted to nicotine, you are always addicted to nicotine. That does not mean that you never get over the withdrawal symptoms; you'll get over those in a relatively short time and may suffer surprisingly few ill effects. Rather, "once an addict, always an addict" means that if you ever indulge yourself in a tobacco product, you'll be immediately "hooked" again—at the same level as you are now. It is very important that you realize this. If you smoke two packs a day and you quit now, if you try a smoke even twenty years from now, you will probably be back to two or more packs a day within a day or two! Your addiction is no different from that of an alcoholic or a hard drug junkie. One drink and an alcoholic will go right back to being a drunk; one snort and a coke head will go right back to being a hard drug user; and one smoke, chew, or snuff and you'll be right back to the habit level you just quit. That is what addiction means. You are a tobacco addict, and you must never forget it! This is not a moral judgment but statement of a physical and biological fact. Addiction will not be a problem for you unless you expose yourself to the ingestion of nicotine at some time in the future.

Psychological Dependence

Psychological dependence is more a state of mind and will probably cause the least of your problems in quitting or staying off of tobacco products. Think of psychological dependence as a child's security blanket. You may have a real fear of giving up tobacco because you *think* you can't get along without tobacco—just as a child has a fear of going out without his security blanket or going to bed without his teddy bear. This is caused by a lack of confidence or fear of failure. You will get over this aspect of your need for tobacco about as quickly as you'll get past your tobacco withdrawal symptoms—in a matter of a few days. Psychological dependence is more likely to show itself as an anxiety over not having a pack of cigarettes where you can get to them easily than as anxiety over being deprived of your smoking. It is something like an angina patient who has an attack because he realizes he doesn't have his nitroglycerine tablets with him. Just having them in his pocket where he knows he can get at them if he needs them is enough to hold off many attacks. That is what psychological dependence means. Confidence is essential to overcome psychological dependence.

Habituation

Habituation, or simply, *habit*, is your toughest obstacle, and we will recommend strategies to help you overcome the habit systems you have built up through the years around the practice of smoking. Habituation involves all the personal "triggers" you've developed over your entire smoking life that say to you, "You need a nicotine fix right now!" Understanding these triggers and being forewarned about them—so that you can recognize them and avoid them—is your best key to remaining a nonsmoker.

Your addiction, psychological dependence, and especially habituation mean that kicking the smoking habit will not be easy, but it is far from impossible. Since it is nicotine that you are addicted to, we do not believe in using smokeless cigarettes, nicotine gum, nicotine tablets, or other chemical crutches. All they do is keep your addiction and habit system alive. To be free of your addiction means to stay away from nicotine in all forms!

It is important to realize that more than forty to fifty

million smokers have quit their habit, and so can you. Many of those millions of ex-smokers regularly smoked two, three, or four packs a day. They were just as addicted as you are. They were just as scared to make the commitment to quit as you are. Their craving for the next smoke was just as strong as yours. They took as much pleasure from smoking as you did. They too decided enough was enough. Something finally motivated them to quit, and that motivation helped them to succeed. Motivation is the key to success in anything we achieve. Motivation in your effort to quit smoking must be stronger than your desire to take up smoking once again. Let's examine some of the motives for you to resist smoking forever.

Facts About Smoking and Health

You've probably heard all the facts about smoking and health before. But now there's a difference. Now you're a nonsmoker. Now you may find it easier to accept the facts regarding the dangers of smoking. When you were a smoker, denial was easier than acceptance of these facts. Now that you're a nonsmoker, let's review them one more time and really think about them for a change.

Actually, the dangers to your health are probably not your strongest motivations to quit tobacco. It has been too easy for you to think or say, "It won't make much difference if I quit next month or next year!" Sound familiar? Well, it does make a difference. Tomorrow, next week, next month, next year, will never come. You'll always put it off for another period of time. The only way to be sure you'll quit is to QUIT SMOKING NOW! Not tomorrow, not next week, not next month, not even after your next cigarette. It has to be now! That's why you are no longer a smoker. You have already quit! You did it now! You're committed!

You've made your investment and have become a non-smoker! Your next smoke would be an end to that important commitment!

Yes, your smoking up to now has injured your health with every single cigarette you smoked. Each one hurt you! Each one did serious damage to your health! Yes, quitting will help you regain good health. And yes, the earlier you quit, the more good health you will regain. It makes a big difference when you quit. *Now* is the best time to quit!

What Does Smoking Do to Smokers?

Despite the denials of the Tobacco Institute, smoking is a serious hazard to human health and life. Up to 500,000 Americans die each year as a direct result of their smoking habit. It doesn't matter if you smoke cigarettes, cigars, a pipe, or chew, tobacco eventually will kill you if you return to it! Smokeless tobacco kills too. Chewing tobacco and snuff—tobacco in any form—is poison to human tissue, and poison kills!

The tobacco industry is the only industry I know of that shamelessly kills off up to 500,000 of its best customers each year. More amazing is that its customers don't seem to mind, they just keep supporting the industry that's killing them.

Yes, tobacco kills tobacco users. Let us count the ways:

1. Smokers die younger than nonsmokers. In fact, the death rate of smokers of all ages is higher than for nonsmokers. And that accelerated death rate climbs significantly in direct proportion to the number of cigarettes smoked, the number of years of smoking, and how early an age the smoker began the habit. This means that smokers in their twenties have a higher death rate than

nonsmokers in their twenties; the same is true in the thirties, forties, fifties . . . and the death rate for smokers accelerates at a much more rapid rate as each decade passes.

2. A little smoke is deadly too. Men who smoke less than a half a pack of cigarettes a day have a death rate sixty percent higher than nonsmokers. A one to two pack a day smoker has a ninety percent higher death rate than a non-smoking peer. Two or more packs a day smokers have a death rate 120 percent higher than nonsmokers in their same age groups.

3. This translates into over 1,300 unnecessary deaths each and every day of the year in the United States alone. That is like five jumbo jets carrying more than 250 passengers apiece crashing every day and killing everyone aboard. This is more deaths in the United States each year than the total of all alcohol-related deaths, drug-related deaths, accidental deaths, murders, suicides, and deaths caused by war in any one year added together. Think about that! What kind of a value system allows such an industry to continue? What kind of mentality keeps people supporting and defending such an industry? Why aren't we as outraged at the tobacco industry as we are about other environmental issues? Tobacco smoke is the greatest environmental hazard in the entire world!

4. Smoking is the major risk factor in heart attacks. Heart attack is the major killer disease among Americans. The American Heart Association estimates that twenty-five percent of all fatal heart

attacks are caused by smoking. That means 170,000 heart attack deaths per year in the United States are caused by smoking!

5. Lung cancer is the second most frequent cause of death among smokers, killing 130,000 Americans yearly. On the other hand, lung cancer is relatively rare among non-smokers—virtually nonexistent—unless that nonsmoker lives or works with heavy smokers. The incidence of lung cancer increases directly with the quantity smoked.

6. Smokers die of emphysema at a much higher rate than nonsmokers. Smokers also suffer a much higher rate of bronchitis, pneumonia, upper airway infections, allergies, colds, flus, sinus infections, and other lingering respiratory illnesses compared to nonsmokers. These diseases not only can cause lingering deaths, but also can cripple a person to the point where she cannot care for herself, be productive, or enjoy even the simplest of life's pleasures. The death toll from chronic obstructive lung disease is about 50,000 Americans per year.

7. Smokers have about five times the normal risk of dying from mouth cancer. Smokers suffer almost ten times the risk of dying from cancer of the larynx. Smokers also have a far higher incidence of dying from cancers of the urinary bladder, pancreas, breasts, and almost every other part of the body. Now aren't you glad you are a nonsmoker?

8. If you or anyone around you is pregnant and you smoke, the chance of having a miscarriage, a stillbirth, a premature baby, a sick baby, or a baby with birth defects is significantly higher. A recent

study has shown that seventy percent of all Sudden Infant Death Syndrome (SIDS) tragedies occur in cases where the mother smoked during her pregnancy and in a high incidence of the remaining thirty percent, the mothers were exposed to smoking by spouses, coworkers, or other acquaintances.

9. Smoking can dangerously increase your blood pressure. High blood pressure is a major cause of brain hemorrhage, stroke, kidney disease, heart disease, and other potentially crippling or lethal diseases.

10. Smoking aggravates and increases the incidence and severity of ulcers, diabetes, hypertension, angina, headaches, migraines, epilepsy, allergies, renal diseases, colon cancer, irritable bowel syndrome, gum diseases, dental problems, and many other health problems. When a smoker gets sick, smoking may dramatically reduce the beneficial effects of prescription medications or the accuracy of medical tests. It is estimated that up to fifty percent of all hospitalizations in the United States are tobacco-related. Think then how much smokers are costing you, a nonsmoker, in added medical insurance costs. Not only do smokers use hospital facilities more than nonsmokers, their hospital stays are longer and require high-tech facilities such as cardiac care, intensive care, bypass surgery, cardioversion, heart pump, emergency room resuscitation, long-term hospitalization, oxygen therapy, lung surgery, or long-term nursing care, that send costs spiraling. We nonsmokers are subsidizing the high cost of smokers' medical care through high insurance premiums.

The list goes on and on. Add them all together and the deaths from tobacco use soars to half a million Americans each year. Think what it must amount to the world over.

If Not for You, Then Be Considerate of Others!

A more tragic statistic than the fact that smoking kills a half million smokers per year is the fact that side stream smoke kills up to 50,000 nonsmokers each year! If you smoke in the presence of others who are nonsmokers, you contribute to the deaths of up to 50,000 innocent people who have made the choice not to smoke. It is this danger to nonsmokers that is causing all the strife between smokers and nonsmokers. If a smoker wants to risk his life and health by smoking, he has that right, but smokers do not have the right to impose danger on people who do not want to breathe side stream smoke. Side stream smoke is not just an unpleasant nuisance. Side stream smoke—the smoke that comes off of the lit end of a cigarette, cigar or pipe, polluting the air all around the smoker—is a lethal air pollutant to all who are forced to inhale it. Most susceptible to these lethal gases and chemicals are unborn fetuses, infants, children, and the elderly.

Side stream smoke is far more deadly and poisonous than the mainstream smoke that the smoker inhales! How is this possible? When a cigarette, cigar, or pipe is smoldering, you will notice the lit portion is a gray color. Its temperature is around only 250 degrees. The smoke pollution coming off its lit end and filling the air around it is cool and contains thousands of lethal chemical components. When the smoker draws on the cigarette, cigar, or pipe, the rush of air passing through the lit end suddenly brings it to life with a hot red glow and the temperature jumps up to 1,000 to 1,200 degrees. Burning is far more efficient at 1,000 degrees than at 250 degrees. At the higher temperatures, many of the lethal chemical parts are burned up so that less of them are in the smoke coming off the burning tobacco. Therefore, side stream smoke has up to ten times more tar, ten times more carbon monoxide, fifty times more benzine, and many more times all of the thousands of poisonous chemical substances that have been analyzed in tobacco smoke.

The Silent Child Abuse

Child abuse has gotten a lot of press in recent years, as well it should. It's a fortunate thing that the media has brought this horrible problem out of the closet. Yet there is a form of child abuse even more far reaching than the recently publicized form, and what's worse, it is perpetrated by people who dearly love their children and grandchildren. Most perpetrators of this silent child abuse would be shocked to realize how serious the effects are.

The silent child abuse usually begins even before the birth of the victim. Physicians are lax in warning against it even when they recognize its signs. This silent child abuse involves the exposure to children of both first hand and side stream smoke. Tragically, parents, grandparents, relatives, acquaintances, and strangers who smoke are constantly assaulting our young. Knowingly or unknowingly, smoking in the presence of children, born or unborn, is nothing short of child abuse!

Child abuse caused by smoking in the presence of children does both physical and mental damage that is too often irreversible. Let's take a closer look at the effects of what we call side stream smoke. Side stream smoke is smoke we are exposed to when we breathe the air contaminated by smokers in our vicinity. Volumes of evidence are now available showing that side stream smoke is a tremendous hazard to our health—and a far greater hazard to children, whose bodies are growing and whose cells and organ systems require a greater supply of fresh clean oxygen to develop to maximum potential. Retardation to development in these maximum growth stages can never be made up for in the future. If you, as a parent or grandparent, expose your children to side stream smoke, you are harming your child's health and future potential. If you are a nonsmoker, but still take your children into areas where they are exposed to the smoke of others, you are also harming them.

Side stream smoke is devastating to children. Let's take a look at some facts:

- The Environmental Protection Agency (EPA) has stated, "Side stream smoke is deadlier than the primary smoke inhaled by the smoker!" Over four-fifths of the smoke from the cigarette goes into the air around the smoker. The side stream smoke contains a measurably higher concentration of cancer-causing compounds than the mainstream or smoker-inhaled smoke. Studies have shown conclusively that side stream smoke contains seven times more carbon monoxide and tar and fifty times more ammonia than the smoker-inhaled mainstream smoke.

- Carbon monoxide blood levels of nonsmokers double when exposed to smoke—even in a well-ventilated room. One smoker in a well-ventilated room will raise carbon monoxide levels to more than double the maximum allowed by the federal government for industrial workers.

- It takes several hours for the blood levels of carbon monoxide to return to normal after a person is exposed to the side stream smoke of just one cigarette. If in that time he is exposed to additional smoke, the levels continue to rise. A child who is exposed to the continuous smoking of a parent, relative, or stranger may never clear the excess carbon monoxide—or 4,000 other harmful chemicals in tobacco smoke—from his small body.

- Yale University School of Medicine has reported that nonsmoking women whose husbands smoke more than twenty cigarettes a day are over one hundred percent more likely to die of lung cancer than the wives of nonsmokers. There are no figures for children yet, but the harm is probably far greater.

- The lungs of children exposed to side stream smoke do not grow as rapidly as those of children who are not exposed to smoke.

- According to the New England Journal of Medicine, children whose parents smoke or who are taken into smoking areas regularly face increased risk of such breathing disorders as allergies, emphysema, and bronchitis.

- According to a paper presented at a Joint American-Canadian Chemical Society conference, an adult nonsmoker who is in a smoke-filled room for one hour will inhale as much cancer-causing materials as a smoker would after inhaling up to thirty cigarettes.

- Smoking is harmful to a developing fetus in a pregnant woman. No pregnant woman should smoke. A nonsmoking pregnant woman should never allow herself to be exposed to the smoke of her spouse or others. Side stream smoke may be even more hazardous to a pregnant woman than if she smoked herself.

• Recent studies have shown that Sudden Infant Death Syndrome (SIDS), or crib death, is related to smoking. Seventy percent of the mothers of SIDS cases smoked during pregnancy. Of the thirty percent who didn't, a great majority were exposed to the side stream smoke of their husbands or others in their daily environment.

• Up to 50,000 nonsmoking Americans will have their lives shortened this year because they regularly inhaled side stream smoke. More than 5,000 will die of lung cancer alone, the rest will die of chronic lung disease, hypertension, heart disease, and other ailments and terminal diseases caused by smoke to which these innocent people and children are being exposed.

• The EPA has stated that "cigarette smoke is the most dangerous airborne pollutant because it contains radioactive particles that cause cancer." The organization also estimated that the lethal effects of side stream smoke are ninety times greater than asbestos.

To the above facts, the American Tobacco Institute states, "The side effects of second-hand smoke are 'negligible and quite small.'" William Awlward, spokesman for the Tobacco Institute said, "If you accept that the National Institute of Health study is (even) close to the truth, then you must also accept that (second-hand cigarette smoke) is not a health issue, but a nuisance issue." When 50,000 innocent people die each year due to inhaling someone else's smoke, it is indeed a "nuisance!" Ask someone who has lost a loved one if it is just a "nuisance issue."

The above are facts you can accept, or like the Tobacco Industry, you can discount them. If you want to continue to court death and illness, that's your business, but when you do your smoking in the presence of non-smokers, it becomes the serious business of others. You have every right to destroy yourself, but you have no right to harm others while doing it.

Hopefully, adult nonsmokers will speak up for themselves when assaulted by the lack of consideration of a smoker. But what about the child who is brought into a smoking area by parent, grandparent, or other guardian? Or a child who is constantly being subjected to side stream smoke by a thoughtless, uncaring parent or grandparent who will insist on taking her own pleasure in spite of the hazard it presents to the child? This is nothing less than a silent child abuse!

What should be done to prevent this silent child abuse?

- If you are a parent or grandparent, quit smoking! Not only will this keep you from contaminating the air your child or grandchildren breathe, but it will also prevent you from setting a poor example. Children learn by emulating those they love and respect. Don't give them a deadly habit to copy.

- If you've convinced yourself you can't quit, then at least don't smoke in the presence of children. In fact, do not smoke in the space they will occupy for at least three hours before they arrive, and then ventilate the space thoroughly.

- Do not ever take a child into a smoking area of a restaurant. In the hour it takes you to eat that meal, the child may get the equivalent damage of smoking two packs of cigarettes. Would you offer any child two packs of cigarettes?

- If children live in your home or visit there frequently, never smoke in your home or let anyone else smoke there. Carcinogens have a way of hanging around in the air.

- Do not take children into buildings where smoking is prevalent.

- Speak up when someone else's smoke is polluting the air you have to breathe. Be insistent if your child has to breathe it. Would you allow someone to serve you or your child a glass of dirty water? Dirty air is far more harmful.

- Become active in movements to provide us with clean air and a smoke-free environment.

Reasons to Quit Other Than Health

There are other reasons to quit smoking in addition to health factors. If your own health and the health of your loved ones isn't enough to turn you away from smoking forever, consider the social reasons to quit.

It is ironic that most of us started smoking for social reasons. Our peers did it, and so we did it to be part of the gang. Peer pressure is the major reason for starting to smoke—that, or seeing our parents or grandparents do it. Now we find that peer pressure is one of the strongest reasons for quitting the smoking habit. All of a sudden, popular opinion has turned against the smoker. Smoking is no longer "in." It has become an antisocial habit.

Smokers are in a minority in the United States today. Depending on what part of the country you are in, what economic level you are part of, and what your educational level is, the percentage of smokers ranges from twenty to thirty-five percent. In any situation, nonsmokers far outnumber smokers. The higher the economic and educational level of your peers, the lower the percentage of smokers you'll encounter.

What social factors make a smoker a less desirable companion?

If You Smoke, You Smell!
Most smokers can no longer detect the acrid odor on themselves or other smokers. If you want to know how you smell to those nonsmokers around you, stick your nose deep into a dirty ashtray full of old cigarette or cigar butts and inhale deeply through your nose. That's how others smell you, even at a distance of several feet. When a smoker enters a smoke-free room, all the nonsmokers in that room know a smoker has just entered, even if she isn't smoking at the time. Your odor precedes you when you smoke. Your breath smells of stale tobacco, your skin smells of stale tobacco, your hair smells of stale tobacco, and your clothes reek of stale tobacco. Now that you're a nonsmoker, take a long shower, shampoo your hair, and get your clothes cleaned. You'll notice people will be more comfortable around you. Also avoid others who smoke, because if you're around them very much, you'll pick up their smoke odor from the side stream smoke.

After you've been a nonsmoker for a few days, your sense of smell will gradually return. You'll slowly begin to recognize the odor in your car, your home, in your clothes closet, in your dresser drawers, and you'll especially recognize it on other smokers. That is what you've been smelling like for as long as you've smoked. While we're on the subject, let's dispel a myth about fragrances. Let's discuss pipe smokers a moment. It seems every pipe smoker thinks his pipe smells wonderful. That's because pipe smokers can't smell their own smoke. So they go out of their way to get the most aromatic tobacco they can buy—they think to add to the pleasure of others. Well, that isn't really the way it works. To nonsmokers and other smokers, there are few odors more offensive than the pungent smell of aromatic pipe tobacco. Most people will agree that pipe smoke is even more disagreeable than cigar smoke. There is a reason why many places that allow smoking will not allow cigar or pipe smoking. Burning tobacco stinks!

If You Smoke You Make a Poor Impression!

When you smoke around nonsmokers who don't know you, their first impression is that you are inconsiderate of others, you have poor judgment, you're of weak character, and you're a fool! And maybe those nonsmokers who do know you think many of the same things. It's hard to respect a person who smokes in face of all the reasons not to smoke. Smokers are indeed fools! Most are indeed inconsiderate of others! Smokers do indeed demonstrate poor judgment! Anyone who has quit the habit himself and those who never fell prey to it are bound to question the character of one who insists he "just can't quit!" Now that you have quit, stay quit!

If You Smoke You're Hurting Your Business!

You probably can't begin to imagine how much business you've lost, sales you haven't closed, or overhead you're causing by smoking. It's one thing smokers tend to deny. Well, let's open your eyes!

You alienate nonsmoking clientele when you smoke.

Unless you own a tobacco store, about seventy-five per-cent of the general population do not smoke. They don't like to be near you because you have an unpleasant odor. If you smoke in your place of business, they do not like to enter it. Nonsmokers want to breathe clean air. If you allow smoking in your store, your merchandise reeks of tobacco. Nonsmokers do not want to purchase items that smell of tobacco, from sales people who also reek of tobacco, or from a store filled with air that smells of stale tobacco.

You increase overhead dramatically when you smoke in the workplace. Government figures bear out the fact that each smoker costs his employer $4,500 more each year than a nonsmoker. This is due to increased insurance premiums, decreased production, lost time from work, increased cost of building and equipment maintenance, and other increased overhead costs directly related to smoking. Companies that do not employ smokers can often save twenty-five to thirty-five percent on health, fire, and life insurance premiums. At today's insurance costs, that in itself is a tremendous savings in business overhead. Smokers take two to four times as much sick leave as non-smokers in a nonsmoking work place. In a workplace that does force nonsmokers to work in side stream smoke, the nonsmokers also have a much higher incidence of absen-teeism. When you consider the wages paid during such loss of production, that is indeed a heavy expense for employers to subsidize. Furthermore, studies show that maintenance costs can be cut by fifty percent when smok-ing is eliminated from the workplace. Electronic equip-ment requires far less repair and cleaning, interiors do not have to be cleaned as often, furniture does not require cleaning, refinishing, or replacement as often because of burns, windows do not have to be washed as often, and carpeting does not require replacement or patching as often when smokers are kept out. Remember, over fifty percent of all fire losses in this country are caused by careless smoking!

These are the reasons why more and more companies are establishing a policy of hiring only nonsmokers. Now, more and more companies are paying for their employees' participation in smoking cessation programs. Some are giving smokers the ultimatum, "Stop smoking or find a new job!"

One of the biggest employee problems employers face today is the dissension between smokers and their nonsmoking fellow workers. It leaves employers one of two choices: go to the expense of putting in separate smoking areas with independent ventilation systems, or get rid of smokers.

Again, smokers have a significantly higher absenteeism than nonsmokers. The higher incidence of upper respiratory infections, flu and other illnesses is responsible for more sick days. Nonsmokers who are forced to breathe side stream smoke eight hours a day also suffer more allergies, colds, flu and upper respiratory problems. So more and more employers find the easiest and most cost effective solution is to get rid of smoking employees.

Last but not least, more and more often, smoking prevents you from getting into the board room. For many of the above reasons, smoking prevents you from advancement. All things being equal, it will usually be the nonsmoker who gets promoted and moves up the ladder. If you recall, statistics show overwhelmingly that the higher the economic and education level of individuals, the less likely they are to smoke. Look around you at the executives in the top echelons of your organization. You'll discover a very small percentage of them smoke. Peek into the executive board rooms. There is seldom smoking there. Few still allow ashtrays. The writing is on the wall.

What Are Your Reasons for Quitting?

The above are but a few of the good reasons to quit smoking. We have yet to find any good reasons for continuing the habit! But there are many more reasons for quitting. What are your personal reasons? Make a list of them. Your reasons are the most important ones. They are your best motivation. Put down as many of them as you can after our listing and review them daily:

1. My health.

2. The health of my family and friends.

3. My job and professional goals.

4. Opinions of others.

5. Economics.

6. I'm sick of being badgered by nonsmokers.

7. My family and friends are worried about my health.

8. I know I've got to do it sooner or later. Now is the time.

9. I'm tired of being a victim and slave to the tobacco industry.

10. _____

11. _____

12. _____

13. _____

14. _____

15. _____

Make It As Easy As Possible for Yourself!

There are a number of tricks to help you keep from ever smoking again. Here are a few:

- Get rid of all your smoking paraphernalia, including cigarettes, cigars, pipes, humidors, pipe stands, lighters, ashtrays, pipe cleaners, and other gadgets.

- Tell others that you have quit smoking and gain their support.

- Take it one day at a time. Just make sure you don't let temptation get the best of you today. Tomorrow will take care of itself. Each day becomes easier than the last, so if you can make it through today, tomorrow will be easier. After the first two days, just forty-eight hours, it becomes a lot easier. It takes about that long for the addiction craving to wear off.

- Remember, it may take only forty-eight hours for the addiction cravings to wear off, but it takes only one cigarette to get you hooked again!

- Avoid other smokers while they are smoking. Their side stream smoke will injure your health and retard your recovery from your own smoking. Additionally, their habit may increase your temptation in the first weeks of your new lifestyle. Just excuse yourself from them politely while they have their smoke. If they are at all considerate, they will not smoke in your presence.

- Try to get others you know to give up smoking along with you. It is easier to "kick the habit" with a friend or a loved one.

- Watch others who still smoke—from a distance. Watch how they are slaves to their habit. In a few days, you'll be able to notice how they smell. Observe how nonsmokers tend to avoid them while they are puffing away.

- Every time you think about smoking, put the cost of a pack of cigarettes away in savings toward a trip or other luxury you'd like to have, perhaps a gift for someone you care for.

- Carry sugarless chewing gum and chew whenever the urge to smoke hits you. If you don't like chewing gum, carry some celery or carrot sticks with you. And don't worry about gaining weight because you stopped smoking. We'll take care of that in the next part of this program.

- When you feel the urge for a brief smoking break, go to a nonsmoking friend and spend a few minutes visiting. Talk about your urge, and give your friend a chance to help you get over it.

- If you can, take a brisk walk after meals when the urge for a smoke is often strongest. Exercise is an excellent, healthy way to get over or avoid a smoking urge.

- Spend as much of your spare time as you can over the next few weeks in places where smoking is forbidden, such as museums, movies, galleries, visiting nonsmoking friends, etc.

- By the same token, for the next few weeks avoid places where smoking is prevalent, such as bars, pool halls, restaurants without nonsmoking sections, etc.

- Try to avoid alcohol for the next few days.

Smoking and alcohol seem to go together, and furthermore, alcohol can lower your resolve. You may need all the perseverance you can muster for the next few days.

- Throw a nonsmoker's party in a couple of weeks to celebrate your victory over a bad habit. Send the invitations now. That will make your resolve stronger.

- Other ideas to help you keep from smoking:

_____

_____

_____

_____

_____

Triggers to Smokers

There are some common triggers that say to the smoker, and to you the ex-smoker, "Now I'd like a smoke." Let's look at some of them, unmask them, and show you how to respond to them or avoid them altogether.

These triggers are not part of your addiction to nicotine; they are part of the habit of smoking. The solution to the problems they cause is to replace them with new habit systems—healthier habit systems.

I miss a smoke after a good meal!

- Leave the table after the meal and take a brisk walk for about fifteen minutes. That's about the time you'd have spent with your smoke. Walking is healthy and aerobic, and it will dramatically decrease your urge to smoke.

- Get up from the table and brush your teeth.

- Chew some sugarless gum.

I miss having a smoke when I get a work break!

- Take a brisk walk, outside if possible.

- Take your break with other nonsmokers.

- Drink some fruit juice, tomato juice, vegetable cocktail, sugarless soda, ice tea, water, etc. Drinking tends to reduce the urge to smoke as long as you avoid coffee, alcohol, or other hot drinks.

I get an urge to smoke when I have a cup of coffee!

- Take your coffee break with other nonsmokers.

- Reduce the amount or avoid coffee altogether for a few days.

- Replace coffee with fruit juices, vegetable juices, sugarless gum, or a brief exercise break.

When I'm under pressure I get a desire to smoke!

- Remember that tobacco does not help you to solve your problems.

- When you have a problem, take the time to thoroughly analyze it, then get away from it for a short while by switching to some other subject, taking a long walk or another form of exercise, or just sitting and daydreaming. Walking, exercising, or daydreaming lets your right brain take over, which is the creative side of your brain. Most great ideas and accomplishments come from right brain activity.

When I watch television, I automatically get the urge for a smoke!

- Reduce the amount of television you watch for the next week or two.

- When you do watch TV, watch with nonsmokers.

- Do not allow smoking in your home or have any smoking paraphernalia available.

- Go to movies, plays, lectures, museums, or other places where smoking is not allowed, instead of watching television for a few weeks.

When I see others smoking, I want to join in with them!

- Avoid smokers for the next two weeks. Spend more time with nonsmokers and let them know you have just quit. They will be only too happy to help you, and you'll probably make some good new friends. Remember, eighty-five percent of all smokers want to quit their habit. They will also be willing to help you if they are true friends. And if you're a true friend, you'll help them to quit too.

Playing cards gives me a yen for a smoke!

- Don't play cards for a while.

- Play cards with nonsmokers.

- Make it table rules that there be no smoking in the room where you play. To make that easier to enforce, be willing to host the game. If the players don't go along with your table rules, find a new game.

When I'm alone or feeling lonely, I want a smoke!

- Now that you're a nonsmoker, you'll find it easier to make new friends. Spend more time with people; seek out new activities.

- Take long walks or other forms of exercise.

- Kill time in places where smoking is not allowed, such as art galleries, museums, movie theaters, the library.

  When I talk on the phone, I get the urge to smoke!

- Avoid the phone! Keep conversations short when you do have to call someone.

  When I have a conflict with someone at home, at work, or anywhere else, I feel like smoking!

- Seek a rational solution to the conflict. Smoking does nothing to resolve a problem. Talk it out. If nothing seems to break the deadlock, stop the discussion for a while. Take a long walk. Change the subject. Give the right brain a chance to resolve the conflict.

  As soon as I sit down in a car, I want to smoke.

- Remember, smoking in a car, even with the windows down, is like riding in a gas chamber.

- Try to take a nonsmoker in the car with you.

- If it's a short trip, consider walking or biking.

- If it's a long trip, consider taking public transportation for a few weeks.

- If it's a regular drive, like driving to work every day, consider car pooling with nonsmokers.

- Thoroughly clean the inside of your car and make it a strict nonsmoking vehicle. Never let anyone smoke in your car. Never ride in someone else's car while she smokes. It's lethal!

  I get the urge to smoke when I'm in a restaurant!

- Never go to a restaurant that does not offer a nonsmoking section and always insist on being seated as far away from the smokers as possible.

I get the urge to smoke when I'm in a bar!

- Stay out of bars for the next two weeks.

I'm Afraid That If I Quit Smoking I'll Gain Weight!

Most people do not gain significant weight when they quit smoking! There is some evidence that smoking may speed up metabolism a little, but it is not usually the act of quitting that causes those who do gain to put on weight. It is typically the practice of replacing the smoking habit with a snacking habit that causes the weight gain. Snacking at its worst is far healthier than smoking. You would have to gain about seventy-five pounds over your ideal weight to put your health at the same risk as smoking.

The Myth About Excessive Weight Gain When You Quit Smoking!

Most ex-smokers do not replace their nicotine habit with excessive snacking. That's a myth the Tobacco Institute loves to see perpetuated. Many smokers, especially women, are afraid to quit for fear of gaining too much weight. To make sure you don't fall into the snacking habit, let's give you some common sense tips.

I'm afraid I'll nibble and snack all day in place of smoking!

- Carry sugarless gum or mints to use in place of candy and other high-calorie sweets.

- Keep celery and carrot sticks available to munch.

- Drink tea, coffee, tomato juice, vegetable juices, unsweetened fruit juices, or bouillon in place of high-calorie soft drinks and colas.

- Other low calorie snacks that you should keep available are tomato wedges, green pepper strips, fresh mushrooms, cauliflower bits, radishes, turnip slices, and cucumber slices.

I get an urge to eat when I'm under stress. Those were the times I used to smoke!

- Find other stress-reducing activities, such as walking or other forms of exercise.

- Practice defensive food shopping. Don't stock up on high-calorie, high-sugar, high-fat foods. If they're not in your refrigerator or cupboards, you won't be able to snack on them. On the other hand, make healthy snack foods readily available. Among these are raw vegetables, fresh fruits, unbuttered popcorn, unsweetened juices, bouillon, tea, coffee, diet drinks, and sugarless gum and candy. Carbonated water is excellent to drink over the rocks or to mix with fruit juices as coolers, making the fruit drink's calorie content even lower.

Quitting smoking is no excuse to gain weight! Weight gain is no excuse for not quitting smoking!

Find and Use a Support Group

How does a support group help you? It is easier to do anything when you have the support of others. We all like to be cheered along and rewarded for our successes. And when the going gets a little tough, the helping hand and encouragement from a friend can do wonders. That's what a support group is all about. Quit Smoking Now! offers you support now, and weeks, months, or years from now. Review this material frequently. It will strengthen your resolve. Let friends, family, and loved ones help you. And in a support group, you'll be helping others, too. That's important. When you help others who are trying to quit smoking, it's virtually impossible for you to backslide.

Regaining Your Health

Your past smoking has damaged your health. If you return to smoking at any time in the future, that damage will continue at an accelerating rate. If you never smoke again, your health status will improve considerably. But the fitness program outlined in this book can help you dramatically speed your health improvement. With some relatively simple changes in your lifestyle, you can get yourself into the best physical condition you've ever been in, recover from much of the damage you've done to yourself, and add productive, quality years to your life. A lifelong smoker will live about eighteen years less than his nonsmoking peers. That is a lot of life wasted. By quitting now you will save many of those eighteen years for yourself and your loved ones to enjoy. You've already done the most important thing by quitting smoking and avoiding other people's side stream smoke!

In addition, this simple program to get you back into shape will also prevent you from gaining weight because you stopped smoking. Follow this program and you'll be in the best shape you've ever known.

Glossary: Simplifying All That Nutritional Jargon

You needn't be a nutritionist or a Ph.D. to successfully develop nutritionally sound eating habits for yourself. The more you know about the language of nutrition, the easier it will be to understand the fundamentals of healthy eating. That is really what we are talking about here: healthy eating habits vs. unhealthy eating habits. If you have healthy eating habits you need never again worry about that ugly buzz word, "d—t"!

The better you understand the language of nutrition, the better equipped you'll be to shop properly and defensively. There is a lot of deception in the labeling of foods because much of the language of nutrition has been created by the marketing people of the food industry. Words such as "natural," "organic," "low sugar," "salt free," "light," "low sodium," "no cholesterol" can be deceptive and confusing on labels, and more often than not, they are that way on purpose.

A big part of understanding nutrition is learning its special vocabulary. Let's take a look at the meaning of special nutrition terminology and thus arm ourselves to make wise decisions about our eating habits.

The Vocabulary of Nutrition

Absorption: the process of transforming nutrients and water from the stomach or intestinal tract through the walls of the digestive system into the blood after digestion.

Amino acids: organic compounds made up of the elements carbon, hydrogen, oxygen, nitrogen, and in some cases, sulfur. Amino acids are the building blocks of proteins.

Additives: chemicals added to food to enhance appearance, taste, texture, and in some cases nutritional value. Preservatives are the most common additives and are used to retard spoilage and prevent growth of disease-causing micro-organisms.

Ascorbic acid: vitamin C.

Biochemistry: the chemistry of animals, plants, or all living things.

Bioflavonoid: a substance found mainly in the pulp of citrus fruits and once named vitamin P. Most authorities doubt its nutritional value or need. Health food manufacturers often hype this substance as beneficial.

Biotin: one of the B complex vitamins. It is widely distributed in foods and is rarely deficient in humans.

Bran: the tough, coarse, and indigestible fiber coat of grains. Since it is not absorbed into the body, it has no nutritional value. Bran is extremely important to health for its mechanical role in digestion and the elimination of harmful byproducts of digestion and other biological functions.

Brewer's yeast: a high-quality protein source rich in vitamins, phosphorus, and iron.

Bulgur: cracked wheat retaining its bran, germ, and nutrients.

Caffeine: a chemical compound found naturally in many foods such as coffee, tea, and colas, which has a stimulating effect on many people.

Calcium: an elemental mineral essential to bone structure, blood clotting, muscle tone, proper nerve transmission, and other biological functions.

Calorie: a unit by which heat is measured; the amount of heat required to raise the temperature of one gram of water one degree centigrade. It thus becomes a valuable measure of the energy source value of food. If a person consumes more calories than are needed to provide the energy demands of his lifestyle, the excess calories are converted to fat for storage.

Carbohydrate: a group of organic substances containing carbon, hydrogen, and oxygen and designated as simple or complex. Simple carbohydrates are sugars; complex carbohydrates are the starches. Both are essential nutrients found abundantly in grains, fruits, starchy vegetables, and milk. One gram of carbohydrate will produce four calories of energy.

Carbon: a chemical element present in all organic substances or substances derived from living organisms. Compounds not containing carbon are classified as inorganic or derived from nonliving sources.

Carcinogen: a substance capable of causing cancer.

Carotene: a carbon-hydrogen compound that occurs in many vegetables and is a form of vitamin A that has cancer-retarding properties as an anti-oxidant.

Catalyst: a substance that speeds or enhances chemical reactions, as in digestion, but is itself not used in the reaction; enzymes are catalysts.

Cell: the minimal, microscopic, functional structure of animal or plant life.

Chemical additives: synthetically compounded substances added to processed foods to enhance their flavor, color, texture, or preservation.

Cholesterol: a constituent of animal fat that is produced in the body, mainly by the liver, and is essential to many body processes and life itself. The body is capable of producing all the cholesterol it needs, so heavy ingestion of dietary cholesterol in animal fats can lead to excessive deposits of cholesterol onto the walls of blood vessels, creating potential circulatory blockage. The greatest danger of these fat or atherosclerotic deposits is their potential contribution to heart attack and stroke. Excessive cholesterol has also been tied to certain cancers. Cholesterol can be divided into high density (HDL) and low density (LDL) lipids. HDL is "good cholesterol" while LDL is "bad cholesterol." HDL, when it is present in sufficient quantity, can protect the body from LDL. Thus it is important to have a low ratio of LDL to HDL. This ratio is more important than the cholesterol count itself.

Cruciferous vegetables: members of the cabbage family that are high fiber and potentially protect against certain cancers. This includes vegetables such as kale, cauliflower, broccoli, and brussel sprouts.

Culture: micro-organisms such as yeasts, molds, and bacteria used to produce cheeses, fermented foods and drinks, buttermilk, and breads.

Curd: the semisolid that forms when milk is exposed to acid or certain enzymes; the semisolid part of cottage cheese.

Dietetics: the applied science of nutrition as used in the feeding of people.

Digestion: the breaking down of food into its simple components in the digestive tract so that it can be absorbed into the body and utilized.

Endosperm: the starchy portion in a kernel of corn,

wheat, or other cereal grain, from which refined flour or meal is produced after the germ and outer fiber layers are removed.

Enzymes: catalysts.

Factor: any chemical substance found in food, nutrient, or non-nutrient.

Fat: an essential nutrient of plant or animal origin. Only about one tablespoon of unsaturated fat is needed daily for good nutrition. Fat supplies nine calories of energy per gram, making it twice as fattening as carbohydrate and protein when ingested in excess. Fats can be divided into "saturated" and "unsaturated."

Saturated fats are most often derived from animal and dairy foods and are usually hard at room temperatures, like butter and lard. Saturated fats tend to raise the bad LDL cholesterol levels of the blood and are considered nutritionally unhealthy whether they come from animal or vegetable sources. Coconut oil and palm oil are vegetable fats that have properties similar to saturated animal fats. Although they do not have cholesterol, they do tend to raise blood cholesterol when ingested.

Unsaturated fats, such as polyunsaturated fats and monounsaturated fats are liquid at room temperature (oils) and are usually vegetable in origin. They tend to lower bad LDL cholesterol while raising good HDL cholesterol. Some vegetable fats have been treated chemically (hydrogenated) to solidify them at room temperature, as in the case of margarine. This reduces their health benefits considerably. Unsaturated fats when hydrogenated take on the unhealthy characteristics of saturated fats. Monounsaturated fats (canola oil and olive oil) tend to lower LDL and raise HDL. But they are still fats and should be used sparingly. When you have to use fat, canola and olive oil are the two you should use.

Fat-soluble: substances that won't dissolve in water but dissolve in fats and oils. Vitamins A, D, E, and K are fat soluble.

Fiber: the indigestible substance in our foods, usually originating from plants. Fruits, vegetables, and grains are all rich in fiber if it is not processed out. Most Americans consume about half the recommended fiber for good nutrition; about 30 grams is healthy. Eating more fiber controls digestion and the elimination of waste and toxins from our bodies, helps reduce cholesterol absorption, and decreases the risk of certain types of cancer.

Folic acid: one of the B complex vitamins essential to our nutrition. Deficiency will lead to anemia and blood disorders.

Fortified: food that has had nutrients added to make it more nutritionally valuable than in its original state. Milk is usually fortified with vitamin D.

Fructose, levulose, fruit sugar: There is a misconception that fruit sugar is not as fattening as refined sugar or sucrose. Fruit sugar is about seventy percent sweeter than sucrose or table sugar, so you can get the same degree of sweetness with about thirty percent less calories, but fructose, when eaten in excess, has similar properties to table sugar.

Germ: the part of grain that grows and allows plants to reproduce themselves. Germ is rich in vitamins and oils.

Glucose, dextrose, blood sugar: glucose is the body's main energy source. It is the main fuel for brain and muscle. Carbohydrates are the body's best source for glucose because they are easily converted into glucose. For this reason, low-carbohydrate d—ts are dangerous.

Gram: the basic unit of weight in the metric system. One ounce = 28.35 grams. One pound = 453.59 grams.

Honey: a sugar compound made up of fructose, a

trace of glucose and a few trace minerals. It is sweeter than sucrose per calorie, but has no health benefits over table sugar. Although it requires a few less calories to get the same sweetening power, honey is more damaging to teeth and has been known to cause lethal botulism poisoning in infants.

Health foods: a very loose and overused term generally taken to include "naturally grown" or "organically grown" foods, as well as vegetarian foods, special dietary foods, foods especially high in nutritional value, and foods produced free of chemicals and additives. All these poorly defined words, terms, and phrases offer no guarantee that these "health foods" are any better for you. The only guarantee is that they are probably more expensive than the "non-health foods."

Hydrogenation: the addition of hydrogen to any unsaturated fat, usually a vegetable oil. Hydrogenation is the process by which oils are changed into solids, such as vegetable oils being changed into margarine.

Inorganic: chemical compounds that do not contain the element carbon and thus are not derived from once living material.

International Unit, IU: a measure of vitamin potency.

Lactose: milk sugar.

Lecithin: a fatty substance found in soybeans, corn, egg yolk, and other plant and animal tissues. Lecithin has the property of being able to dissolve cholesterol deposits in the body. Our bodies are capable of producing lecithin in varying amounts, which may explain why some of us are more protected from high cholesterol than others.

Lipids: another term for fats, fat-like substances, and oils.

Light, Lyte: a marketing term that implies fewer calories or fat in a product, but in no way guarantees this.

Macrobiotics: a diet based on whole grain foods.

Microbiotic: pertaining to microscopic plants or animals such as bacteria, molds, and yeasts.

Minerals: inorganic substances (vitamins are the organic counterparts) that are essential to life. Iron, potassium, calcium, zinc, iodine, copper, phosphorus, sodium, and chloride are a few of the essential minerals we need for health and life maintenance.

Natural foods: a loosely defined term that usually means food produced with minimal processing, refining, and no additives or produced with no chemical fertilizers, hormones, pesticides, or antibiotics. The label "natural," however, does not guarantee any of the above.

Nutrients: substances needed by the body for life and health that cannot be produced by the body itself and thus must be obtained from foods we eat.

Organic: those chemical compounds that contain carbon and that are obtained from living or once living matter.

Protein: an essential nutrient made up of amino acids and necessary for tissue growth and repair. Protein derived from animal tissue is usually complete, containing all the essential amino acids. Plant protein is usually incomplete and must be eaten in combinations of vegetation to be as nutritional as animal protein.

Preservatives: chemicals that inhibit spoilage or growth of micro-organisms. Preservatives are particularly important where proper refrigeration or freezing are not available.

P/S ratio: expresses the relative amount of unsaturated fat to saturated fat in oils or margarine. The higher the number, the higher the amount of unsaturated fat the product contains. Thus, the higher the P/S ratio number the healthier the product.

Riboflavin: vitamin B2; one of the B complex vitamins.

Roughage: Fiber.

Salt: the common name given to sodium chloride or common table salt. Most Americans consume far more salt than is needed by the body, partly because of its excessive use in food processing. Salt is associated with increased blood pressure in people at risk for hypertension.

Sodium: a mineral found in many foods and the inorganic element that combines with chloride to form common table salt. It is sodium that causes hypertension when excess salt is ingested by those at risk for the disease. Some present studies indicate that sodium in forms other than table salt are not as likely to cause hypertension. A person should limit her sodium ingestion to less than 3000 milligrams/day.

Starch: the complex carbohydrate found in grains, potatoes, and vegetables, as opposed to the simple carbohydrates, such as sugars.

Sugar: the simple carbohydrate found in fruits and other plants. Sugars have very little nutritional value other than providing flavor and calories.

Vitamins: organic substances derived from plants and animals that help to regulate metabolism and body functions. There are thirteen required vitamins, each with several unique functions in life processes. The fat soluble vitamins A, D, E, and K can be stored in body fat so they needn't be eaten on a daily basis. The water soluble vitamins C and B complex cannot be stored and must be included in our daily nutrition.

This glossary of basic terms is not intended to make you into a nutritionist, but it should help you to understand labels, advertisements, and marketing ploys a little more. More importantly, it should help you to understand better what might be harmful in your nutrition, what is good for you, and what won't help or harm you. The basic idea of nutrition is to avoid what will harm you, seek out what is good for you, and enjoy or ignore the rest as you see fit. If you are interested in a deeper understanding of nutrition, I refer you to your local library which will have dozens of books on the topic. I remind you to ignore the section of books on diet and stick to the section on nutrition. There is a big difference between the two.

Helpful Organizations

AAA (American Auto Association)
Check directory for local phone listing.
Emergency road service, trip planning, maps, insurance, etc.

Alzheimer's Association
800-621-0379

American Aging Association
University of Nebraska Medical Center
Omaha, NE 68105
Research and information on aging.

American Association of Retired Persons (AARP)
1909 K St., NW
Washington, D.C. 20049
Check directory for local phone listing.
Lobby organization that also provides insurance, discount pharmaceuticals, support groups, and information.

American Diabetes Association
800-ADA-DISC

American Foundation for the Blind
800-AF-BLIND

American Geriatric Society
10 Columbus Circle
New York, NY 10019
Information on aging and health.

American Heart Association
7320 Greenville Ave.
Dallas, TX 75231
Check directory for local listing.
Information on lifestyle change to prevent heart disease and stroke.

American Kidney Fund
800-638-8299

American Paralysis Association's Spinal Cord Injury Hotline
800-526-3456

American Social Health Association's National STD Hotline
800-227-8922
Information on sexually transmitted diseases.

American Society on Aging
833 Market Street
San Francisco, CA 94103
Check directory for local listing.
Research, information, representa-
tion, resource center.

American Speech-Language-
Hearing Association Helpline
800-638-8255

Arthritis Foundation
800-283-7800

Asthma and Allergies
Foundation
800-7-ASTHMA

Aviation Safety Institute
800-848-7386
Health and safety tips.

Cancer
Cancer Information Service
800-4-CANCER

Dentists for the World
303-758-5405
e-mail: DTTW@AOL.com
http://rwsa.com/VTTW/index.html
For dentists wanting to do volunteer
work in the United States and
abroad.

Doctors to the World
303-748-5405
e-mail: DTTW@AOL.com
http://rwsa.com/VTTW/index.html
For medical personnel wanting to do
volunteer work in the United States
and abroad.

Elderhostel
100 Boylston St., Suite 200
Boston, MA 02116
617-426-8056
For those over 55 wishing to travel

and learn.Offers courses on all sub-
jects all over the world.

Epilepsy Foundation of America
800-332-1000

Foster Grandparents Program
c/o Action
Washington, D.C. 20525
Volunteer aid to youth in need

The Gray Panthers
3635 Chestnut Street
Philadelphia, PA 19104
Check directory for local listing.
Lobbying, information, research,
resource center.

Hospicelink
800-331-1620

Impotence Information Center
800-843-4315

Lung Line Information Service
800-222-LUNG

National AIDS Hotline.
800-342-AIDS *(24 hours)*

National Citizens Coalition for
Nursing Home Reform
1424 16th St., NW, Suite L2
Washington, D.C. 20024
Lobbying, research, information,
watch dog agency.

National Council on the Aging
600 Maryland Ave., SW
Washington, DC 20024
202-470-1200
Lobbying, information, research,
resource center.

National Council on Alcoholism
and Drug Dependence Hotline
800-475-HOPE *(24 hours)*

National Council of Senior Citizens
1511 K St., NW
Washington, D.C. 20005
Lobbying, information, research, resource center.

National Domestic Violence Hotline
800-333-SAFE *(24 hours)*

National Head Injury Foundation
800-444-NHIF

National Heart, Lung, and Blood Institute
301-496-4236 (*Information office*)

National Hospice Organization
1901 N. Port Myer Dr., Suite 402
Arlington, VA 22209
702-243-5900

National Institute of Aging
900 Rockville Pike
Bethesda, MD 20205
Lobbying, information, research, resource center.

National Organization for Rare Disorders
800-999-NORD

National Rehabilitation Information Center
800-34-NARIC

Older Women's League
1325 G St., NW
Lower Level B
Washington, D.C. 20005
Lobbying, information, research, resource center.

Organ Donation Hotline
800-24-DONOR *(24 hours)*

Parkinson's Educational Program
800-344-7872 *(24 hours)*

Prostate Information Line
800-543-9632

Saga International Holidays, Ltd.
Park Square Bldg., Suite 1162
Boston, MA 02116
Trips and tours of interest to and designed for older travelers.

Vista/Peace Corps
c/o Action
Washington, D.C. 20525
Volunteer opportunities in the United States and abroad.

Volunteer Tour Programs
303-758-5405
e-mail: DTTW@AOL.com
http://rwsa.com/VTTW/index.html
Volunteer opportunities in the United States or abroad.

Volunteers to the World
303-758-5405
e-mail: DTTW@AOL.com
http://rwsa.com/VTTW/index.html
Volunteer opportunities in the United States and abroad.

Widowed Persons Service
Dept NB
AARP Programs Dept.
1909 K St., NW
Washington, D.C. 20049
Lobbying, information, research, resource center.

YMCA
Check directory for local listing.
Actvities, fitness programs, support, etc.

Index